DEVELOPING PEDAGOGIES IN THE MULTILINGUAL CLASSROOM
The writings of JOSIE LEVINE

DEVELOPING PEDAGOGIES IN THE MULTILINGUAL CLASSROOM
The writings of JOSIE LEVINE

selected and edited by

Margaret Meek

Trentham Books

First published in 1996 by Trentham Books Limited

Trentham Books Limited
Westview House
734 London Road
Oakhill
Stoke-on-Trent
Staffordshire
England ST4 5NP

© Original sources (listed on p.xi)

British Cataloguing in Publication Data
A catalogue record for this book is available from the British Library
ISBN: 1 85856 067 5

Designed and typeset by Trentham Print Design Ltd., Chester
and printed in Great Britain by Bemrose Shafron (Printers) Ltd., Chester

Contents

WAYS AHEAD

Publisher's Note

When Josie Levine and Margaret Meek first approached Trentham Books with their proposal for this book I was delighted. For one thing, Josie had recently remarked that Trentham was the house with which she would like to be and now there was a way to realise her wish. For another, we had just finished one demanding and hugely rewarding project together – Josie had guest-edited the Spring 1996 issue of the journal *Multicultural Teaching* – and I was sad that our collaboration had ended. Josie has been a joy to work with – 'a very good editor', as she herself said, but also warm, fun and wonderfully celebratory of the achievements of her contributors.

Trentham is non-profit-making but our books still have to pay our way, and this is another reason for my enthusiasm. Josie was so far ahead of her time that her ideas on teaching and learning English as an additional language are wholly relevant to teachers today. This book will serve another generation of teachers as her work has done for two decades.

With Josie's declining health, a first-rate editor with her own expertise in children's learning was needed. That it should be Margaret Meek – co-editor of *The Cool Web* and of Trentham's *First Steps Together* – is a publisher's dream come true! This book is our tribute to a brave and wonderful woman and fine, empowering teacher, and it is a treasure-trove for teachers working with children for whom English is not their first language.

Gillian Klein
July 1996

Although we raced to produce this book, Josie Levine did not live to see it. It is a testimony to the sharing creativity she maintained to the end and a celebration of her life-long achievement.

Trentham Books

August 1996

Acknowledgements

Jose Levine's papers are usually to be found near the scene of action in teaching and research, to be picked up and read by those they are designed to help. My first thanks, then, are to Josie, for agreeing that her papers could be brought together, then in equal measure to all those who found copies for me, and to others, whose permission was needed and granted, notably Jean Bleach, Hilary Hester and Malcolm Clarkson. Josie's and my friends and colleagues at the Institute of Education, especially Jane Miller, gave to us both much encouragement and practical help. The Director, Peter Mortimore, arranged for us to have the splendid support of Lorna Barker. The collaborative skill and expertise of Gillian Klein at Trentham Books and John Stipling and his team at Trentham Print Design made this book possible.

x

Sources

1. 'Voices of the Newcomers': original title 'Children from Families of Overseas Origin' by Josie Levine and Alex McLeod in *Language and Literayv in our Schools; some appraisals of the Bullock Report.* ed. Harold Rosen. Institute of Education 1975 pp35-49

2. 'You Liar, Miss', from *Changing English; essays for Harold Rosen* ed. Margaret Meek and Jane Miller. Heinemann Educational, 1984

3. *Scope, Stage 2,* is part of a paper published in the *International Review of Applied Linguistics* Vol XlV/2 May 1976

4. 'Developing Pedagogies for Multilingual Classes' first appeared in *English in Education* Vol 14 No 3 Autumn 1981

5. Originally, 'Potential of a Language Model for Bilingual Pupils: Match and Mismatch' with Jean Bleach, is one of a series of papers, *Lessons in English Teaching and Learning,* published after a NATE conference held on June 25 1988 to discuss proposals for the teaching of English in the national curriculum.

6. From *Issues in Race and Education*, Language and Learning. Summer 1983

7. *Project Papers No 4,* with Jean Bleach. (Second Language Learners in the Mainstream Classroom Project) ILEA, Hackney and Islington, January 1986

8. From *New Readings* ed. Keith Kimberley, Margaret Meek, Jane Miller. A&C Black 1992

9. *From Charting the Agenda: Educational Activity after Vygotsky.* ed H.Daniels. 1992 Routledge

The quotations at the beginning of each chapter (except Chapter 3) are taken from Bilingual Learners in the Mainstream Classroom edited by Josie Levine, Falmer 1990.

Introduction

Even after almost half a century of acknowledging, with varying degrees of hostility or acceptance, the presence of ethnic minority groups in most urban areas of Britain, many people are still uncertain about how best to respond to the presence of children from these groups in school. They are expected to learn English as an additional language, often without appropriate recognition of the fact that many of them are already bilingual, and that none of them should be expected to abandon the language and the culture to which they owe a primary allegiance. Yet, there is no doubt that without the full participation of these young people in schooling, the population as a whole would face far-reaching social and economic consequences and greater dilemmas than how to teach them.[1]

Most countries where English is the dominant language have common concerns about 'linguistic minorities'. It is generally agreed that learning to speak and to write in English is more than a matter of technical competence in the language. In addition, it involves learners in the discovery of how to develop and present a broader personal identity and to express a range of understandings derived from more than one culture. As the result of much thought and social action, especially by teachers and other educators, there is now more general agreement that where linguistic diversity is part of the constructive base for the development of a school curriculum – where it is 'counted in' rather than discounted or ignored – children's bilingualism is a not a problem. But this is only a beginning.

The really important issues surrounding bilingualism and additional language learning are not confined to schooling, although schooling is bound up with broader social decisions about equity and entitlement as these are construed within the larger structures controlled by finance, power and class as provision for the regulation of diversity more generally. But it is in school, where children are expected to learn English, that the strands of all other issues, historical, political, pedagogic, affective and developmental — in matters such as literacy and access to higher education, for example — come together. It is also where important distinctions have to be made: for example, that children learn English not before anything else, but *as* they learn everything else.

This book touches on all of these topics. It consists of a selection of papers written by Josie Levine (occasionally with friendly collaboration) for her students and colleagues about the teaching and learning of English as an additional language. The papers are presented here to acknowledge and honour the work of their author, and also to introduce a new generation of students and teachers to the origins and development of some of the most significant ideas that now inform the understanding of language in an education system that is bound to take account of diversity and difference if it is to provide adequately for *all* children.

On this occasion, however, the treatment of these ideas is experiential, facultative, empowering. It begins in classrooms, with the interaction of pupils and their teacher and returns there, but not before a number of conventional beliefs, practices and dogmas have been searched, destabilised even. As the ideas emerge from an altered context, new situations and conditions for children's ways with words, we learn different lessons about social and intellectual inequalities, as well as more about English as a modern language.

Begin then, as you read the first two chapters, where Josie Levine began to engage with this topic in the 1960s. At this time there was nothing 'trendy' about class teaching where no precedent was available for the resolution of the teacher's dilemma about how to help her new and recently arrived pupils. Her resources were her own intelligent listening, her imagination, and the children's determination to communicate with her and with each other. Often, children who don't speak English but, as

2

yet unknown to anyone in school, are already fluent in two other languages and perhaps also literate in one, have had searing experiences unknown to others: a long journey, serious displacement as the consequence of war, changes of climate, languages and culture. In Josie's class, what their teacher records is their resilience, their determination to learn by exploiting every iota of language competence they can support with gestures, body language and words they hear in the streets and, sometimes at the beginning, the listening silence. Where no immediate transformation of their language seemed likely without material resources in the classroom, their teacher could have despaired. Many did. Instead, Josie collected *evidence* of what the children could do with help, and even on their own, as they struggled to say what they had in mind.

From hundreds of such initial encounters, teachers have grown in understanding that classrooms are social communities. They support, or they may inhibit, children's coming to know their new world. As the pupils tackle their new language Josie 'counts in' their feelings, full-sized as they are, as the energising force of their learning. Certainly, first-stage learners need explicit teaching in the nature of English itself, from talking and listening to tutoring in reading and writing. But, just as necessary are the possibilities the teacher gives the pupils for communicative action, doing things together, talking about the job in hand, and seriously discussing topics of empowerment. The phrase 'where is fair?', asked of her by one of her pupils (see Chapter 2) became central to Josie's thinking and thus to this book. It packs into the smallest space the layered meanings and challenges presented by the children, who will not be fobbed off with notions of resignation, conformity or compliance.

The first lessons bring about changes in teachers as listeners. They hear new voices, different ones, and in their turn, they learn from the pupils enough to be amazed at the transformational speed of their new linguistic competencies: what they have to say and how they say it. But the content of the saying is also different as it comes from the differently situated background and perspectives of the speakers. Teachers are also realists, however. They know that between four and seven years will pass

3

before the beginners they are so proud of can be assured that their English will match their learning to the satisfaction of the gate-keeping examiners.

In the early days, teachers who had classes with children learning English as an additional language sought each other out to exchange information and experience, to study language itself, even to learn something of the languages the pupils already knew, and to make suitable materials when these were not forthcoming or adaptable from elsewhere. These self-chosen groups of proto-specialists extended the domain of socio-linguistics by offering different kinds of evidence. The learning context was not simply in school but all around outside it, throughout all the media of transmission, notably television, films and books. In addition to their teachers, children had other models and sources for their practice and learning. How strange it now seems that this was less than obvious at the time – even deliberately ignored.

This teaching and learning grew, as the saying goes, from the bottom up. Teaching and learning English as an additional language in multilingual multicultural schools acquired its theoretical backing from the teachers' analyses of their practice, especially in their scrutiny of language captured by tape recorders. No matter how current policy makers now formulate their exalted perspectives on this chapter in the history of education, the fact is they were slow to *celebrate* linguistic diversity, one of the key educational issues of the second half of this century. Events could have taken another turn. During the seventies, the Schools' Council supported materials making initiatives for teaching English and bilingual pupils, notably *Scope, Stage 2* (Schools Council, 1972). Later, when the Council was disbanded and another project, Language for Learning organised by Jean Bleach and which called on the expertise of teachers, came to an abrupt end, Josie's informal support group had already collected enough evidence to further a more wide-spread understanding that all children who needed to use English as an additional language should have full access to mainstream education. Some of that documentation became part of the evidence influential in persuading the Department of Education's Committee of Enquiry into the

Education of Children from Ethnic Minority Groups (the Swann Committee), to be 'in favour of a move away from E2L provision being made on a withdrawal basis, whether in language centres or separate units in school'. Josie's view is: 'This was one of those (rare) occurrences in education when a policy shift and an innovation can truly be said to have derived from the groundwork of teachers themselves'.[2]

Whereas members of most professions continue their learning from the on-going processes of research in their field, teachers have no such guaranteed resource. They are expected to become their own experts by exploiting a range of relevant documentary sources and, more particularly, to conduct their trials by means of action research from the ongoing interactions in their own classroom, from reflections on their interactions with pupils and discussions with colleagues. They are granted 'training days' and meetings. They pay the fees for their advanced studies. Often their results are considered by practitioners in 'exact' sciences to be 'insufficiently rigorous', but the practice of ethnography and the support of anthropologists like Shirley Brice Heath have removed many of the boundary markers between formal and informal research procedures. Read another way, teachers have changed the rules of evidence.

The period covered by the papers in this collection came just after intense activity in language studies. The spin-offs from other social, historical and cultural studies, together with a growing interest in the psychology of Vygotsky increased teachers' confidence in classroom evidence as significant. At about this time – halcyon days in my recollection – Josie and I were collaboratively responsible for a group of teachers who were studying the role of language in learning. They had a year's secondment from school to explore the new research and to consider how the findings might influence their teaching. Josie introduced a specialist module for those who wanted to study more intensively the teaching of English as an additional language. The teachers' research exercises in this context were described by Josie as 'learning through acting on' what they taught their pupils and what they wrote and read. They are still some of the most highly regarded practitioners in this field, not least because their

5

secondment year gave their specialist interest the impetus and the breadth it needed.

Later, as the drive to put in place a national curriculum with its emphasis on tests, targets and league tables intensified, the feeling tone of the time changed and became inimical to the progress of those children who needed longer than their monolingual peers to reach the criteria set for the Key Stage of their age group. Again, teachers had to work harder than ever to make this inequality obvious in the short time allowed for revisions of the Orders. Over the decade that has followed the institution of the National Curriculum it has become clear that Josie and her colleagues had discovered and promulgated effective pedagogical practices from which there could be no turning back. You will find them detailed in these pages: mainstreaming, partnership teaching and action research. There are other things too, on which it would be helpful to gloss: ways of checking on the efficacy of materials and resources designed for learners; means of assessing children's core knowledge which may be masked by their struggles to express themselves in English; but I believe the examples speak for themselves.

At no point in Josie's presentation of her ideas is there any minimising of the teachers' and the learners' difficulties or of their recurrent bewilderment. Nor is there any exclusion of how learners feel about their chances of success, nor about what they want to say or write or the texts they read. The importance of books offered to children learning English lies not only in their quality and relevance as learning materials. They also convey to the readers the nature and extent of their teachers' belief in their ability to learn. There is still a longway to go. Professional practice in this kind of teaching is constantly in evolution, linked as it is to teachers' observations and the unspoken premises derived from what Geertz calls 'the sheer actualities of experience'[3.]

In these pages you will also find an inspirational teacher who has always set high standards for her colleagues and students. She has done this in a number of ways, including intervention in public debate about official findings, (the Bullock Report, 1975, the Swann Report, 1985 and the Cox Committee proposals for the English Orders in the National Curriculum, 1988) and by writing and editing stories and books for inexperienced readers of English. Undeniably, her influence on the teaching and learning of children and teachers has been paramount. The evidence in contemporary classrooms makes that plain..

I remember how, in the early days of our acquaintance, I was jolted by Josie into an almost cosmic awareness that I had led a sheltered life in mainstream English teaching (I didn't know that's what it was at the time), by avoiding the school of hard knocks of inner-city realities and the challenges of linguistic diversity (with the exception of a boys' high school in Leeds). Sometimes I felt simply defective, in my ignorance of many Black writers, the intricacies of racism and the privations of the inner cities. Josie and the teachers she worked with undertook my education and earned my undying gratitude. She also showed me how powerful and how easy it was to 'dispose' of children who did not fit the 'normal' categories, just by using the category system itself, and how damaging a legacy categorisation of children bequeaths to us (Levine, 1990 p.13). Over more than two decades of generous co-learning and friendship, I discovered what teaching and learning could really and fully be like: continuous, collaborative, intellectual and imaginative inquiry, amongst other joyous things, involving parents, teachers, researchers and our splendid colleagues, to discover and work on how best to help children to learn, and to provide the means of their success; while at the same time to wonder why teachers are held responsible for the defects of a system they are not encouraged to change, when, given the opportunity, they could do just that.

The papers in this collection were published first in a number of places listed on page xi. To bring them into this framework I have borrowed, with permissions, quotations from Josie Levine's writings in *Bilingual Learners and the Mainstream Classroom* (Falmer Press, 1990), which appear under the title of each chapter.

Margaret Meek, London, June 1996

Notes

1. I am indebted to the SCAA Discussion Paper no 5, January 1996: *Teaching and Learning English as an Additional Language: new perspectives* and for the opportunity to be present at the international conference from which the report came.

2. Department of Education and Science, 1985 *Education for All: The Swann Report* HMSO p 392, quoted in *Bilingual Learners and the Mainstream Classroom*, ed J. Levine (1990) Lewes, Falmer Press.

3. Geertz, Clifford (1983) *Local Knowledge; further essays in interpretive anthropology*. New York, Basic Books.

STORIES FOR INTERPRETATION:
evidence from the early days

In 1975, the Report of the Bullock Committee on 'various aspects of English' and called *A Language for Life*, brought to the fore the schooling needs of children described as 'from families of overseas origin'. The writers of the Report had been made aware of the complexities of this topic by evidence supplied by teachers, and were careful to say that 'no one should accept a stereotype of 'the immigrant child". They also recognised the long-term issues of additional language learning, urged the special training of teachers in English as a 'second' language, the fostering of home-school links and the maintenance of each child's mother tongue.

The two chapters in this section show Josie Levine's pre-Bullock recognition of children's linguistic competences as they learn English, not only in classrooms but in their daily lives, and demonstrate her subtle sensitivity and openness to their linguistic skills. They are just as apposite for teachers today.

Chapter 1

Voices of the newcomers

In the first instance we were simply but creatively, and against the thinking of the time about what language teaching was, trying to create in our withdrawal situations, a rich language learning environment – one in which our pupils could learn to use English for educational purposes by using English for educational purposes. It was through trying to make our special language classrooms as 'normal' as possible that we slowly began to perceive the potential of the mainstream for our students' development of a use of English. Meanwhile, we first had to argue the case, not for mainstreaming but for this functional-communicative style of teaching (Levine, 1990 p.21).

When the word 'immigrant' first began to appear in the literatures of Housing, Education and the Social Services, someone said, in response to the way in which blame for the prevailing conditions always seemed to fall on the newcomers themselves, that far from them being the cause of the ills, they were, in fact, acting like a barium meal in society, highlighting existing inadequacies and injustices; in education, for example, at all levels – government, local education authority, in administration, in the curriculum and day-to-day activities and strategies in the classroom.

Few people heard, however. To hear was to fly in the face of prevailing feelings about immigrants: that they were not here to stay, or that those who did would become like 'us' once they'd settled down and learned English (and, presumably, changed colour). Most people in a position to make and carry out policy wanted to institute caring, but short-term, reforms that would get things back to 'normal' as quickly as possible. Those who did hear were usually people capable of thinking in multi-ethnic terms, already involved in radical action for change. They recognised that immigrants and their children also had problems and they were susceptible to the following notions:

- that learning is a process different in pace, rhythm and timing for each of us

- that differences among individuals are normal, and so, by extension are differences of race, colour, creed, dialect, background, culture ...

- that the 'hidden' curriculum is learned as surely, if not more so, than the overt one

- that the role of language in education is central, and that one of the most powerful contributions to the learning process is to let learners have their own voice.

At first, these formative and innovatory ideas were far from being either coherent or acceptable. Small wonder, then, that so few teachers understood what was at stake, and fewer still could imagine that multiracial and multicultural awareness would have to be part of a coherent theory of school curriculum development, especially in the teaching of English to bilingual pupils beginning to learn English. We now see what was needed in the early days. Had we understood then what we know now, the consequences would have been different.

There are schools today where too many children (including those who have had initial English teaching on their arrival) have learning problems which are language linked. These children grow in alienation not only because the gap between what they are expected to do and what they can do increases, but also because the attitudes they encounter, to their speech, colour, background and to their apparent failure to learn, tell them they are not rated, not wanted, not part of whatever is going on in school.

There are schools, not in multi-ethnic areas, where children are growing up surrounded by obsolescent attitudes and values derived from a mono-ethnic past. There are teachers who think that there is no need to change either their ways or their curriculum to meet the new demands. ('They came here, didn't they, and what I'm going to give them is good old English education'.) There are teachers who do have goodwill, but who are in difficulties with the children they teach – many of whom are the children of immigrants – because goodwill needs a backbone of deep understanding and skill to be effective.

All of this leads to a number of paradoxes. On the one hand, there are special language service teachers, organised in different ways by local education authorities and always unlikely to be adequately numerous, whose job is to teach English to beginner learners of English as an additional language. These teachers guard their special status and skills, most of which are derived from the model of modern language teaching. But they also want the class teachers to help them in discharging this responsibility for children learning English as an additional language, while at the same time being anxious about the effect of the 'open' English lessons, which seem to run counter to the tenets of specialised teaching of language. On the other hand, teachers in the mainstream of a school are often inhibited by the mystique surrounding special English lessons and reluctant to get in the way of a process which seems to have additional prestige. Some of them also have other reasons for keeping away. Their view of language development is grounded in a psychological theory of personal constructs, which has little in common with skill reinforcement methods of teaching language.

Thus, there is a powerful and ironic clash between mother-tongue teachers and 'special' English language teachers. Yet both groups probably come closer than any others in understanding the role of

13

language in education, and the need for a language policy which embraces the whole curriculum. Further evidence of the factors I have sketched here can be found in the recommendations of the Bullock Report, paras 245-266. (eg 249 'No child should be expected to cast off the language and culture of the home as he crosses the school threshold, and the curriculum should reflect those aspects of his life'. 258 'In the secondary school, pupils who are past the initial stage of learning English need help in coping with the linguistic demands made on them by the various specialist areas of the curriculum. To this end there should be close cooperation between subject teachers and language specialist'). But is it not a sad reflection on our attitudes that it is still necessary to say so many of these things?

We should cease to categorise the education of children of families from overseas origin under headings like Problem or Difficulty, as if it were a branch of education somehow separate from our main business in schools. It is not. The circumstances faced by the children of families from overseas origin and their teachers are the circumstances faced by a majority of children and teachers in urban schools – only writ large.

Put it another way. If we could understand about mixed ability teaching, how, when it is working, the environment is both flexible enough for children to be individuals with a chance of making a worthwhile contribution to the work of the class, and structured enough, in differing ways, to provide each child with the assurance of some success; how, when it is working, contexts vary in order to provide a range of situations in which children must ask questions, discuss and argue, organise, be organised, recount and describe, listen, talk, read, and write to some purpose, work with each other as well as on their own, have the opportunity to find things out from people, from books and pictures and through other media. Then many of the anxieties felt by both teachers and pupils in the 'ordinary' classroom would diminish, and another set of anxieties felt by teachers and pupils in the 'special' language classes would also diminish.

What I am trying to say is that we can expect the structures, organisations, strategies and techniques developed for 'mixed ability teaching' to have something to say for *all* learning and teaching. The term 'mixed ability teaching' like 'multiracial education' is so often linked with 'difficulty', 'problem' and 'underprivileged' that we tend to forget that it is a way of thinking about all teaching situations.

To illustrate what I mean, let us look at just one part of this mixed ability environment; that of letting children have *their own voice*, to see what it can mean for children's language and other development. And let us look at it with the children of families of overseas origin in mind.

At the beginning of this current term (Summer, 1975), a second year class in a north London comprehensive school were asked to write down what they had done in English this year. The children in the class come from a variety of ethnic backgrounds (English, Irish, Scottish, Italian, West Indian, Nigerian, Greek Cypriot, Turkish Cypriot) all of whom, except for one of the Nigerian boys who arrived only a few months ago, have received most, if not all of their education in England. They seem to me to demonstrate *the range of activities taking place in the class* and, amongst other things, *differing ways children have of approaching their work, their differing experience in language related tasks.*

Interesting too, is what they 'choose' to omit. Zekye, for instance, makes no mention of the extremely thick folder of high standard stories and poems which pour out of her. Perhaps it is not surprising. Their number is so great as to be almost daunting. And Chris entirely forgot to mention that he was the one who organised a whole trip to the Arsenal stadium. Like most of us, he needed help to get started, eg the letter of request we wrote together. He was worried about spelling and saying it right, but all subsequent decisions and letters he took and wrote on his own. Altogether, it was a thoroughly competent job which included making a list of those who wanted to go under the names of the teachers whose lessons they would be missing.

One further point should be stressed, namely, the way in which the structure and organisation of these particular English lessons create the freedom for children to be in learning *relationships with each other as well as with their teacher.* Chris, again, provides an example of this happening. He is very friendly with Abdol, the boy newly arrived from Nigeria. They spend a lot of time together both in and out of class. Chris helps him with his work, shows him round, encourages him, makes sure he goes to his special English lessons, and is, in fact, playing no small part in Abdol's reasonably successful adjustment process.

Maria is a year older than the others in her secondary school class because she started infant school a year late. She was born here, but has once done the return trip to the Caribbean. Maria does not have the kind of language difficulties, which, if we are not careful, we can label all Black kids as having. In fact, she is an able, independent, not un-sophisticated girl, sometimes sunny, often in trouble, often sulking and resentful. At the moment she is 'into' slavery. She wrote the following poem at the beginning of the term's work. She is in the process of writing more and has just finished reading *The Slave Dancer* by Paula Fox.

The hunger

Long ago people were led into bondage.
There to remind them that they were slaves
was a cord on a handle, which meant the simplest thing
meant a flogging,
whipped till they were dead,
like weevils that damage crops.
Helplessly the women struggle,
whispering as they work all day.
They were shouted upon.
You weakling, in need of rest already?
With pale look on their faces, they
dare not stop.
You can see the hungry look grow on their faces
Revenge we will take,
and for one day we will gain strength with the help of the Lord.
No more will any human be led into bondage.

No need to comment on the writing. I want simply to note two things. The first is that she has *the freedom to make her entry* into what for some is a contentious issue. It is a freedom which allows her to 'do her own thing' without pressing it upon others, and one which in no way diminishes the quality of work. The second point which I wish to take up is how she came to use the word 'hunger' at all in the poem, for it was not there in the first place. It seems to me to demonstrate both a *capacity for rigour* on her part and also the way in which the *freedom*, which we have previously noted for the child, *acts for the teacher in that it enables her to enlarge a pupil's repertoire at a point in time when it has the greatest meaning for her*. It is the range of intervention that becomes possible within this mode of operation that renders it so productive.

Maria's poem had no title, and the fourth line from the end had read originally, 'You can see the voracious look on their faces'. In her first version, 'voracious' had been put in brackets by her teacher. Maria explained the brackets this way:

> Well, when I wrote the poem, 'voracious' was what came into my head. When I looked it up, it said 'hungry'. And that was my meaning. But when Miss —- read it, she said that 'voracious' meant more 'greedy' than 'hungry' for her. When I looked it up in another dictionary it had 'greedy' in, too. Now I don't know what to do. 'Voracious' sounded so good.

We tried a thesaurus, but with no luck. In the end, she gave up 'voracious' and settled for her meaning, 'hungry'. The title grew out of that.

In passing, she had met and learned how to use a thesaurus and learned, also, something about the classification of words.

> 'What's Adj, miss? Oh, I see. It's a word like hungry.'
> 'Yes. Adjective.'
> 'And N?'
> 'Noun.'

Then, that day, she went back to her typing and quite quietly listening to a reggae tape: part of the gestation period for the very long story – not without merit – which she brought in the following week.

The kinds of intervention a teacher undertakes will depend on the pupils. How they are that day, and, to be clinical, where they are on a national curriculum of language development. In Maria's case, intervention is likely to be of two kinds, the thesaurus kind, and a textual kind. In the case of children like Hari Krashna Patel (the author of '*The Long Journey*' below) it might be the same levels of intervention (eg helping him find his way round an atlas or, perhaps, working on the cohesion of a story or poem, or it could be something quite different, more specific, which has to do with his handling of certain syntactic elements of English).

Here is Hari Krashna Patel's story.

The Long Journey
(I will WRAIT PART TWO FOR you TOMORROW)

DATE/ 20th September *1974*

Joseph. Ali the good man and very cayned man.
He Bournd in 1873. Every one like him.

Every one call him Jose because everyone like to
keep his name Jose.

But Jose don't know in what countery is he living in
and the name of the city. But his friends knew the
name of every countery. they wanted to know that how
good is he at it. Jose was louᶜky boy.

In 1893, Jose was 20 years old. he wated to know
the world. so he ask some of his men to come with

18

him to see the world. One of his men said. Jose but
how are we going to go. we haven't got plain. and haven't
got ships. Jose said so what, we can go by boats.
So every one was ready to go. Jose was sitting alone
but his men said to the women that we are now
in Brazil and we were in colombia, we walked some
where in Amazon valley. when they got to South Arica,
they have some rest and got some food. at last they
talled Jose that we are in South Africa now, and we want
to go to AUSTRALIA. Jose said o.k. you want to go.
we will all go together. they went from South Africa to Ethiopia.
in Ethiopia they were in trabal they were keeped in Prisenar
for One year. by sailing and sailing. Jose got older and older.
He was 89 years old when they reached Australia.
Jose can not live any more.

So he give his plase to his bast friand Richard.

On fourth day after his Birthday he daid on his
fathers bed, he brough with him

he was very good man as his father was
than his frainds were lived for ever

and that
is THE
            END   of PART ONE of JOSEPH
                             ALI.

Hari Krashna Patel goes to another comprehensive school in north
London. He is an experienced user of language, but not yet of the English
language. His fantasy life is almost entirely wrapped up in Indian films,
and like Maria he already sees himself as a writer. At the time when he
wrote 'The Long Journey' he was thirteen and had been in England about

two years. He had gone straight to secondary school as a complete beginner of English, where some of his timetable was, and still is, spent in a special English class strictly geared to learning *about* the English language. His mother tongue is Gujerati.

The Long Journey was not school work. It arose out of a range of writing, taping and other opportunities he gets in an out-of-school group he belongs to. In school, he is one of the liberal sprinkling of children from non-English speaking backgrounds, not long in this country, ready to learn and who have things they want to say, but who are, as yet, inexperienced in using the English language for doing these things, and who need teachers both in 'special' English classes and in 'ordinary' classes who will intervene at affective and structural levels.

Both the piece and the group are relevant to this discussion, since in whatever sense the group does *not* resemble a class in school, it does resemble one in three very important ways. It is mixed ability. The children in it are getting the chance to develop the means to express their voices. The mode of operation, though looser because it is not school, is very close to that at work in the second year class mentioned above.

The Long Journey was a breakthrough for Hari. It was his first lengthy piece of writing, the first without little notes attached apologising for his mistakes (although the apologies came verbally, the first time we met after he had done the writing). It was also the first writing done at home by any member of the group. (He continues to write at home, and two of the others have also started to do this now.)

The day the story got written they had had in school a geography test of the kind 'What is the capital of —?' He did not do too well. ('But Jose don't know in what countery is he living in and the name of the city. But his friends knew the name of every countery. they wanted to know that how good is he at it.')

That evening the group had with them a visitor from South Africa with whom Hari spent a lot of time talking about journeys and travelling. They used an atlas so they could explain to each other more clearly. That is to say, the visitor was showing him how to do this, and in talking about her own experiences was also showing him how to talk about his. Towards the end of their chat, he said:

> 'Miss, is the story of Christopher Columbus true?'
> 'Yes,' we said, not seeking to enter into the niceties of that kind of truth.
> 'OK. I will write you a story like Christopher Columbus, only not true ...
> Miss, I am wanting to borrow atlas. OK?' (Notice how competently he has used the atlas for his story to 'place' Joseph Ali's journey.)

It was a break-through for me, too, in that it gave me the chance to see what he *can* do, what he *does* understand. For example, his feeling for a particular kind of writing, his sense of the ways of men, his ability to transmute experience, his capacity for rigour, the fact that he has a fair grasp of the underlying systems of rules which govern native speakers' use of English.

His feeling for a particular kind of writing: In this case, the epic tale.

His sense of the ways of men: In this case, I would say, of the role relationships in democratic tribal groups. For example:

> 'In 1893, Jose was 20 years old. he wanted to know the world. so he ask some of his men to come with him to see the world. One of his men said. Jose but how are we going to go. we haven't got plain. and haven't got ships. Jose said so what, we can go by boats.
> Jose was sitting alone.
> at last they talled Jose that we are in South Africa now, and we want to go to Australia. Jose said O.K. you want to go. we will all go together.
> Jose can not live any more. So he gave his plase to his bast friend Richard.'

His ability to transmute experience and to use it to suggest the springs out of which the hero acts: An example of this we have met already in the matter of the geography lesson. Connected with this same example is the way in which he takes his own feelings about being ignorant and his own determination to know as much, if not more, than the others, and turns them into Jose's drive 'to know the world.'

His capacity for rigour was first brought home to me in the 'radio' programme he made of the story. As he came, through the means of the taping to revise and expand the story, he found Richard's sudden appearance ('So he gave his plase to his bast friend Richard') unsatisfactory. And on the tape he can be heard muttering 'But who is Richard? We must know who is Richard.'

What he knows and understands about the underlying systems of rules which govern native speakers' use of English, of which we can find out as much from the errors he makes as from what he gets right.

'I will ~~RIAT RITA~~ WRAIT...'
'plase'
'daid'
'every country'
'talled'
'plain'
'He bournd in 1873.'
'Jose'

In his 'radio' programme, this last is always spoken as 'Joseph, and he explained that he wrote it this way to save time. So he is 'into' abbreviations, too.

For some, it might seem that I am arguing for intervention in the affective areas of learning only. But plainly for children such as Hari, such intervention is not enough. They need teaching that is not afraid to deal with structural areas. Such teaching might include these two mutually inclusive strategies (among a great number) for helping in this structural area of language learning. The first is to make sure that certain structures with which he is grappling at the moment, occur regularly in his environment, so that he has something to model. One might say that any learning in such instances was synthesis by osmosis, but not chance. One such structural matter one might decide to take up could be that exemplified in his sentence 'But Jose don't know in what countery is he living in'. The other strategy is a much more direct attack, where the structure of a sentence (or the way of saying something in English) is brought overtly to his attention, talked about and practised. For example, his grasp of the rule for expressing past-ness in English is sound enough to cause him to make errors with less familiar words which do not follow the general rule (he has no errors with the verb 'to know'). This might be a good point, therefore, to introduce some things to do in which the object is to note and practise these arbitrary distinctions.

It is difficult to think of a child who can do all the things Hari can do as an educational difficulty or problem. It is difficult to see how one could have known these things about him except by letting him have his own voice and also by intervening at the affective *and* structural levels of learning. It is difficult, therefore, for me to see how those of us interested in language development, whether we are first- or second-language teachers, can continue productively in our work except if it derives its power from the mode of teaching that I have been attempting partially to describe. That it will appear different in different circumstances I have no doubt.

Chapter 2

'You liar, Miss'

The willingness to struggle to arrive at relative understandings within ourselves and of others, and to express our wishes and ideas, is just as fundamental an ingredient of successful learning and language learning through interaction as is the basis in trust. It is the trust that forms the basis of the willingness to struggle (Levine, 1990 p.139).

It is Friday afternoon a little way into the Autumn term. Ours is the reception class for immigrant children, beginner learners of English at the local secy mod in Handsworth, Birmingham, parliamentary constituency of Sir Edward Boyle, Secretary of State for Education. Boys and girls, only one of them more than a year in the country, all of them from Jullunder District in the Punjab, are sitting comfortably together. It is 1964 and we are an unusual group of people.

Until this time, the handful of bilingual pupils who had come into schools had, apparently, just picked up the language. In our school there were four or five outstanding boys, fluently bilingual, high-fliers, confident. One, who acted as our interpreter, had, in the space of a few short years, taken hold of opportunities for qualification for apprenticeship, and also had so become 'one of us' that the remarkable thing about his speech, so I discovered from what the newly arrived children said, was not so much that he spoke English with a Birmingham accent, but that he spoke Panjabi with Birmingham accent. Teachers were as pleased and proud of boys like Rupinder as they were of their successful indigenous pupils. Certainly teaching them had not threatened their expertise nor created in them a need for change.

It came as a shock, therefore, to find that Rupinder's pattern of progress was not to be general. As numbers increased and children no longer came into classes singly, the concept of mixed-ability teaching hardly having been aired yet, teachers found themselves increasingly at a loss as to what to do and correspondingly resentful of the fact that the sort of teaching they ordinarily did reached fewer and fewer children in their classes. Beginner users of English, now in classes in fives and sixes, found themselves, literally, sitting on the edges of the class, given things to keep them occupied. (Over time, some tens of thousands of houses must have been drawn, coloured and labelled for want of teachers' knowledge of something better to give them to do.)

With teachers so anxious and uncertain then, it was apparent that something had to be done to preserve 'normality'. Nationally, the debate on this centred on numbers: what percentage of immigrant children, culturally and linguistically different from the indigenous population, could be tolerated in a school before the school must necessarily cease to function in its usual ways? Thirty per cent was suggested as the crucial figure in a parliamentary speech of Sir Edward Boyle's (27 November, 1963)[1]. Where this figure was reached, he suggested, immigrant children should cease going to their neighbourhood schools and, instead, be dispersed among other schools. The other proposal for a speedy return to normality was for the newcomers to be taught English on a withdrawal basis, so that when they knew enough English, as received opinion had it, they would he able to take their rightful places in ordinary classes and schools.

Withdrawal teaching of English gained ground. Our school went along with this. Even those of us who some 15 or 20 years later argue for a very different provision for the needs of developing bilingual pupils in our education system could at that time see no other way of fulfiling the obligation to provide all children with an education according to their needs. At that time, we were probably correct in thinking that unless the children were removed from the mainstream in some way, they could only go on being the 'non-learners' they appeared to so many to be, and would increasingly gain the disrespect of their peers and teachers. Certainly, they had to be sheltered from that. With hindsight it is easy to see that our good intentions can also be labelled institutional racism, but the experience and the analysis which now enables us to do so had not yet been developed.

The usual way of organising ESL (English as a Second Language) teaching was for peripatetic teachers to visit about three schools a week and withdraw children for special English lessons. On average, children would attend three lessons a week, for about an hour each lesson. The classes were often made up of children of all ages, with the children put with others from classes different from their own, who were estimated to be at about the same level of English.

We did not do this in our school. I was not a peripatetic teacher but a full-time member of the school's staff Nor did we withdraw children randomly from different subject lessons, the usual way in which the specialist classes were composed. Ours was a full-time, all-age reception class. All newly arrived immigrant children who had yet to learn English came into it. There certainly were advantages in this. We were able to get to know each other, develop, as in all other classes our group dynamics, lay down our own classroom culture, and also have some feeling – small though one has to recognise it was with hindsight – of belonging to the school.

The Head had acted with pragmatism and a certain caring. By now his school had well over 30 per cent immigrant children on roll. If he acted on the recommendation about dispersal his numbers would fall (for no one, of course, spoke of bussing white children to replace the dispersed immigrants). He preferred that his school remain a neighbourhood school, and so it was the impracticality of bussing in Birmingham, if not the outright rejection of the principle, which provided us with some stability. The setting up of our reception class increased that sense of stability.

The children certainly needed it. And so did the teachers. Like almost everyone else in the country doing this work at the time, I was not trained for it. Because mine was a full-time class of mixed ages I was quickly forced to acknowledge that it was not pedagogically possible to do English language lessons all day every day; you don't learn a language *first* before starting to use it. For my first two weeks I tried it – from a highly unsuitable book written for adults that required the teacher to drill the students in sentence patterns. It drove the light out of the children's eyes. Moreover, if the children were supposed to go back into ordinary classes as soon as possible, hadn't they better get to know what they could of some of the subjects taught there? From then on, as far as was possible, we tried to follow a timetable of curriculum subjects in learning English – some parts of which also took in the standard specialist practice of teaching language structures. The children responded to doing school learning and, like all children, to being able to give voice to what they thought and felt, and to the opportunity to ask real questions.

Our group was significantly different, then, both in the way it was organised and in the way it worked, from most other groups constituted for the purpose of learning English as a second language. I did not know enough then about learning or about language learning, or about how to analyse the educational system in which I was working to be theoretical about any of it. I was simply responding to the children's disappointment and to my bright-eyed belief that schools could be enjoyable places to be in if your mind is actively engaged. It was an exploration in communication, accommodation, construing, de-centring, indeed mixed-ability teaching (although, of course, I did not know those words then), an exploration which quite often faltered at the level of initial comprehension, but was seldom characterised by intention to misunderstand.

This Friday afternoon, as always, Santokh Singh and Jai Singh sit side by side in the double desk near the door. Jai, silent, shy, contained, is often the butt of offensive racial and sexist remarks from his fellow Panjabis, because, unusually in their experience, his hair grows in tight curls. Santokh, at thirteen, is small, tough, streetwise; a foot shorter than Jai and two years younger; outgoing, daring, the class spokesman. The class looks to him for the otherwise unthinkable – to challenge the teacher.

Sarwan Singh is there. He had arrived one day with Santokh ('Miss, Miss, new boy. He very clever. Know English very good. You teach him') but was, nevertheless, unable to respond to my basic questions. 'No, Miss, not talk, write. You write, Miss. He know writing', Santokh instructs. So I write *What is your name?* The boy, understanding instantly, takes the chalk and writes beneath my words on the blackboard, swiftly and fluently, *Sarwan Singh*. The whole class smiles with pride and Tarlojhan takes him under his wing, for Tarlojhan – whose name was constantly mispronounced by his teachers – was the guardian of names, insisting, when others of his peers gave up, on respectful attempts by foreigners to say them correctly. Indeed, one of my colleagues considered him an awkward customer on the grounds that he refused her the license to call him Tommy when she suggested it as a solution to *her* difficulties. 'No, Miss, everyone must have right name. No good change.'

This Friday afternoon, Sarwan and Tarlojhan sit together in another double desk, two back from the front against the high-windowed wall. Biro Kaur sits in front of them, next to no one – Kuldip is away today. Biro is supposed to be eleven; more likely she is eight or nine. Everything she does suggests this. She skips and plays round the classroom, distracting the others until they must appeal for help. 'Miss, tell her be quiet. We want work.' Today though, she, like the rest, is sitting quietly, ready to begin.

Besides, Kabel, too, is sitting quietly, at a desk in the centre of the room next to Gurnak. Unusually, Kabel has returned from lunch untroubled by the length of the school day. The calm around him suggests that we shall escape his song of disaffection and, therefore, Biro's dancing accompaniment to it – for Kabel, at twelve years of age, is expert in rhythm and finger drumming, highly skilled in it, and with an evident ability to weld new experience and words into his songs. Endlessly, unstoppable, he sings this song, until his feelings are spent: 'Tk, tk, no good; Tk, tk, no good; Fuck, fuck, no good...'

Gurnak is one of those who call for quiet when Biro and Kabel tell their troubles in this way. He is more explicit about what is going on inside and outside the classroom. The windows of his house brick-broken for the second time, he asks bitter questions. 'What for they do this thing, Miss? My father good man, my mother good woman. Work hard. No make trouble.' And on another day, when I am lecturing them about how they should behave, he challenges me. 'Miss, why you tell us be good all the time? I *am* good boy, Miss. Why I must be gooder than English boy? Why you tell me this, Miss? Where is fair?' I cannot answer. I am shocked to discover how much of what I resented as a kid, but could not articulate, I am unquestioningly asking of them. ('Don't do your homework in the kitchen', my mother once said. 'You'll get grease on the paper, and they'll say "Those Jews are dirty".') Gurnak's question reveals to me that I do not know what to do to act against the racism on the streets, despite the fact that some twenty years before we too had hate and stones thrown at us by other children as we left our (Jewish) school for home each day.

In front of Gurnak, in a desk by himself, sits Dara Singh, tiny, chirpy, namesake of a renowned Panjabi heavyweight wrestler, his hero. Tiny Dara, his desk festooned with posters of Dara Singh, all biceps, torso and thighs, has appointed himself my guardian.

Elsewhere, behind Tarlojhan, Dara's elder sister, Monahan, sits, also by herself but sullen, forced by English law to be there (glad of it I discover months later but then so split by the disparity between wanting to be in school and another felt knowledge, deeper for having been grown up with and still constantly reinforced, that education is not for girls, that even depressive inactivity comes to look like a major achievement on her part).

Jasbir Kaur and Ranjit Singh, sister and brother, newly arrived, sit together, quiet, courteous, watching, alert; no 'Pinished, Miss' from them. Exquisitely trained, they put down their pens, close their books, fold their arms and wait calmly for the next assignment. They do not address me except to answer a question directly put, and then, monosyllabically. But they are not silent children. Anyone can see that from watching their conversations and interchanges in Panjabi. Nor does their 'goodness' and refinement of manners estrange them from the rest of the class, as one might be forgiven for anticipating. However, it becomes increasingly and worryingly clear to me that such exquisitely dutiful behaviour, applauded and approved by almost every teacher, is in effect a barrier to what Ranjit and Jasbir want to learn. Of course, they need time just to become acclimatised and also to grow accustomed to the sound of a new language. But how on earth, I ask myself can they learn to *speak* English if the 'correct' way to behave in class is *not* to talk? I go along with them, though. Shamefacedly, ambivalently, I offer Ranjit *Ladybird Book 6a*, and with the irony that often accompanies these events, he initiates for the first time a dialogue with me. Handling the book like an insulted expert, he says 'OK, Miss, I understand I learn read this book (he meant learn to to read English by using the book; after all he is already a reader in Panjabi)... then you give me good book.

Finally, sitting across the gangway from Jasbir and Ranjit, is Dalbir Kaur, artist and only friend of the silent Monahan. Some months earlier, before she could write English, Dalbir had started to draw marvellous, colourful, descriptive pages. We would sit together as she pointed at the things in her drawings which she wanted named. Little by little stories emerged. I wrote a sentence or two. She copied. Then she began to write her own sentences for the continuing flow of pictures. By the time Jasbir and Ranjit had joined the class, through Dalbir's talents we had found a classroom enterprise that gave us all great pleasure, one worthy of sustained attention. It was our communicative currency, the way in which real incidents and imagined stories, episodes and events from the past were shared; the way we came, in fact, to know each other. It never occurred to me to encourage the use of Panjabi as a learning medium. It was taken for granted that English was the language one had to use in the classroom. After all, I could speak only English, and English was the task in hand: mine to teach and theirs to learn it.

Normally on a Friday afternoon we would be in the gym, dancing and playing games, activities much looked forward to. This was our time for relaxation, a fitting end to the tensions of the week. But this Friday we have a job to do. The children's personal details have to be checked. The Head needs them – at the last moment, of course – and no, Monday, when Rupinder, who translates for us, will be back at school, won't do. The returns have to be made by four o'clock *today* or the school won't qualify for the special government assistance available to schools with immigrant children. I decide not to mind, and rationalise it as a chance to do the sort of English work that will always be useful in the outside world – form filling.

I explain that we have a job to do for the Head, that it shouldn't take long, that after that we can go to the gym. On the blackboard I have drawn a simplified form.

Name _____

Address _____

Age _____ Date of birth _____

Time in UK _____

I ask them to copy the form on to their pieces of paper. This they do. They are attentive.

We do 'Name' first, which is easy. Some *can* read it, of course, and others take the meaning from the *shape* of the written word. Furthermore, they can all write their names. Then we do 'Address'. Again, everyone can either read it or knows the shape; they can all *recite* their addresses, too. Unfortunately (for speedy delivery from this task), they cannot all *write* their addresses. It doesn't matter, though. It's all good practice. I go round helping, and today, such is our rapport, they give the task their full concentration. Today, too, for the first time, Dara is able to ask for help.

'Miss, show me, Miss. You write. I write same.'
'Copy', I say. 'I'll write it first and you copy.'
'Yes, Miss. You write. I write same.'

I walk round, back bent. Many tongues are caught between lips in concentration. I see Jasbir helping Monahan.

'Age' is easy. They all know the numbers. Biro, too, can write 11, even if she can't read 'Age'. But I write it down for her because everyone else has finished. Sailing along now, relaxed, confident, happy. Soon we'll be finished.

> 'Right', I say. 'Date of birth.' I look round for someone I think will
> know. 'What's your date of birth, Ranjit?'
> 'Don't know, Miss.'

I try Jasbir. Same answer. Tarlojhan. The same.

It must be that they don't know the *phrase* 'date of birth'. I turn to Santokh. After all, he is not only *their* spokesman. He is mine, too. He is sure to know, and then he can translate, and Gurnak will get it, too, and then we'll be finished.

> 'Santokh, what's your date of birth?'
> 'Don't know, Miss. What means date of birth?'

Ah! so that is it. They haven't met the phrase before. Our time in the gym recedes. But never mind. I turn to the blackboard, and as an example start to fill in the form with my own details. Name. Address. Age. They become extra attentive and polite when I fill in my age.

'Now, *date of birth*', I say, writing down the year, 1964. 'This is how you work out your date of birth', I say. 'I am 28, so to get the year I take 28 from 1964 and the answer is 1936.' I put 1936 at the end of the 'date of birth' line on the blackboard.

'Now', I say, again, 'my birth *day* is on the fifth of May. That's the fifth day of the fifth month', and as I say it, I write 5 for the day and 5 for the month in front of the previously written 1936 on the 'date of birth' line. 'You understand?' I ask, 'My date of birth is 5:5:1936.'

They smile comprehendingly, for in so far as I have performed for them the meaning of the phrase 'date of birth', they *do* understand. We are all extremely warm and pleased with each other. Delighted, I rush straight to the follow-up. 'OK, so now you all understand *date of birth*?'

'Yes, Miss.' A chorus and more smiles.

'Good, so all of you write down your...' The smiles evaporate. '...date of ...' they shuffle, their attention flying elsewhere. '...your date of birth', I finish, lamely.

They look at each other in consternation.

'Come on', I say. 'It will only take a minute. What's the matter with you?'

'No, Miss. Not understand.' Not understand! What do they mean, not understand! They've just said they *do* understand. Silence. They look down. I look at Santokh.

'Santokh,' and I am speaking harshly, separating the words. 'Do you understand *date of birth*?'

'Yes, Miss.'

'OK, Santokh,' I say, measuring my speech still. 'Then please tell the others so we can write everything down and finish and go to the gym.

'No, Miss.' What?! 'No, Miss. You liar, Miss.'

Anger flashes, and hurt as well. A liar! How dare he! Is there a child who can call his teacher a liar and think he can get away with it? Well, Santokh is one such, obviously. I can hardly breathe, but he, seemingly careless of the effect of his 'insolence', continues in his role of spokesman.

'True, Miss. We not got date of birth like you got date of birth. We can't write answer for you. We not know.'

I breathe deeply. 'But you know how old you are, right?'

'Yes, Miss.'

'So how do you know how old you are if you don't know your date of birth?'

'My mother know. She tell me how old I am. But I not know date of birth.'

I am mystified. I cannot see how anyone can know their age *without* knowing their date of birth. Nor, if I am to be honest, how anyone cannot know their own date of birth. It's *natural* to know one's date of birth. Everyone does. Why are they being so stupid? I try again. 'But you have a passport. What's written in your passport? Your date of birth must be written in your passport.

'Yes, Miss, but not like for you date of birth.' Santokh sighs patiently. 'You not understand, Miss. Nobody writing like here, Miss, when baby is born. When we come England, my mother say my son born when this happen or that happen. High Commission man in India listen, then he write in passport date of birth number.'

I get it. At last I get it. And it is I who feel stupid. It is my mis-understanding, my lack of cultural understanding, not theirs, which is blocking the progress of this lesson. Somehow Santokh must have understood this and decided to get the matter cleared up instead of being resigned to an impasse. Why else would he have called me a liar? He could have said I was wrong. He knows that word, But they had already told me earlier in the exchange with that 'No, Miss. Not understand', that it was *I* who did not understand. Only I had assumed they were telling me that *they* still didn't understand – easily done when the frame you are working in allows you to assume that in the relation between those who know a language and those who are learning it it is always the learners who have to do all the understanding. Locked in my own way of thinking, taking for granted the 'naturalness' of 'date of birth', it must have seemed as though I was *deliberately* not understanding the truth as they knew it to be. Puzzling, too. If they could understand my truth, how come I could not understand theirs? I was their teacher, after all. So, to Santokh, I wasn't just wrong, since you can't be wilfully wrong. He needed something else to convince me that I was in error. 'Liar', when you look at it from his point of view, isn't such a bad try. It has in it the sense of deliberateness he must have been looking for. That he did not yet know that the word 'liar' is specific to *telling* an untruth and not generalisable to *failing to understand* the truth or that he didn't seem to know the force of the common effect of uttering the word, was the result of inexperience in the language, not wilful ignorance, contempt or abuse on his part.

Everyone learning a language, whether it is the first or a subsequent one, takes time to get to know the range of particular words and the limits on their use in that language. Everyone makes 'mistakes' in trying words out, and the more daring you are in these attempts the more you are open to other people's mirth and anger. This kind of risk-taking is much to be encouraged. Sometimes this exploratory use of language creates a poetic phrase like 'Miss, I like best lion's jungle room', following a visit to a zoo, or a classic howler like 'The shits on the bed', in describing a picture in an English language lesson, but it also produces phrases like 'You liar, Miss'. Because of the different, indeed hurtful, ways in which such attempts at communication are often received, many second-language learners never take the risk, preferring to stay within the safety of what they know they know. It need hardly be emphasised that this is a constraint on their learning. Inexperienced users of language, almost more than anyone else (although that, of course, is arguable) need teachers who will both encourage this risk-taking and be willing to go for the intentions behind their words.

Chastened, I continue. 'Good, so you *can* write for me. You can write the date of birth number in your passport.

'Yes, Miss ... er ... no, Miss...'

My consternation returns. 'But I thought...'

'Yes, Miss, but we not have it except for passport, so we not know it, Miss.'

Kabel, ever alert, responds. 'Miss, passport number in register'.

And I laugh. For so it is.

If those of us in education in the 1960s, who questioned its provision for newcomers to this country then, could have been transported to the 1980s we would have been astonished to find how much progress had been made:

* comprehensivisation

* mixed-ability grouping

* mixed-ability teaching

- knowledge about the relationship between talk and learning, based on interactional learning theory and communicative theories of language learning

- ever-increasing knowledge about first- and second-language development

- mother-tongue teaching and maintenance

- bibliographies and suitable books of fiction

- documentation and analysis of racism, classism and gender in education

- anti-racist teaching and multicultural curricula being developed by teachers

- equal opportunities policies introduced in some LEAs, with time-tables for schools to begin implementing them.

In the area of teacher training we would have found students on initial courses of training calling for proper integration of multicultural issues into their education courses, and – at last – being taken seriously; the same students, our next generation of teachers, calling for their subject methods course to prepare them for working with the developing bilinguals they will undoubtedly have in their classes rather than – their words – always leaving the work to specialists. In schools we would also have found teachers, often in partnership with specialist English language teachers, asking questions about their own curricula and teaching methods, and finding ways and means of changing and developing so that bilingual learners can *usefully* learn where they ought to learn best – in the mainstream classroom; and crucial to much of this development we would have found teachers undertaking investigations through which they are not only learning better how to respond to diversity, but also making significant contributions to curriculum development – in fact, becoming their own experts. We would have found too, the concept of everyone, not only those in urban, multiracial settings, receiving an education fitting them for living and working in a multicultural society, and the equating of such education with that of a good, i.e. normal, education.

Achievement indeed. So it would come as a shock to learn that, despite all this, children in the 1980s still and daily experience racism, lack of opportunity and an inappropriate education. Gurnak's cry of 'Where is fair?' reverberates across the years. While the concepts for it are firmly with us, fair curricula which grant to all members of a school community equal access to learning are still to be fought for and made real.

Surely, we could reasonably ask, more should have been achieved than this? Why does it take so long to begin to institute educational changes, the changes in training, curricula and pedagogy which are necessary if we really do aspire to a fair society? First, it is because most initiatives are made in the teeth of an established opposition, which works equally hard and with an equal commitment to maintaining the status quo. Second, initiators work from positions of powerlessness *vis-a-vis* the administering of changes.

A short-term view of the amount of conflict and energy necessary for change in education leads to despair, and every day without change works against people's life chances. It is monstrous that the 'fair' changes we argue for are still so hard to bring about.

An oppositional posture is bound to increase the time that is ordinarily needed for ideas to be developed and for the practice that stems from the theory to be developed. Change does not happen by virtue of one insightful theoretical leap nor by the spread of theoretical ideas alone. Individual teachers have to learn and think about theory, take steps to implement it, reflect upon their practice and develop it. Moreover, each new generation of teachers has this learning to do and needs a climate which encourages it.

The development of new pedagogies for mixed ability teaching – coming out of theories about the relationship between talk and learning, which have been around for some time; and theories of additional language development, which are less well-known in the mainstream of our education system – is an area of curriculum innovation which needs to be strengthened. By putting these ideas into practice on behalf of bilingual pupils language specialists and mainstream teachers, working together, have developed both their strategies for supporting English language learning and better learning environments for everyone. Importantly, groups of teachers are discovering for themselves that talk helps learning and that children becoming bilingual need support across the curriculum (also what that support might be). This learning anew what is already known by some is an important step in teachers' learning about teaching. To be able to state that this will involve both the taking on of collaborative roles between pupils, between pupils and teachers and between teachers, and also in some sense a negotiated curriculum, and then be able to describe how, over time, these conclusions and practices are reached, takes this learning further. It is also, and significantly, a contribution to the *theory* as well as the practice of teaching.

If the insights and practices of this current generation of 'learning' teachers are to take hold we have to continue the fight for conditions that will foster them. Our present ground-base offers hope. We can now say that there is a greater recognition that diversity of need is the norm rather than one standard all-purpose curriculum. But best of all is the fact that teachers are seeing themselves as active participants in the making of curriculum and classroom methodology rather than accepting without question a role as transmitters of received 'wisdom'.

Reference

Sir Edward Boyle, House of Commons, 27 November 1963, Hansard, vol. 685, cols. 433-44 Quoted in E.J.B. Rose et al. *Colour and Citizenship,* Oxford University Press for the Institute of Race Relations, 1969, p. 268.

RECURRENT THEMES

By the middle and later seventies, the teaching and learning of English as an additional language began to influence other aspects of teaching in school. This was noticeable when specialized 'withdrawal,' lessons were gradually transformed by teachers within the language service who had begun to experiment with curriculum-based language lessons. Josie Levine was one of the leading specialists in this new endeavour. She had seen the need to create a linguistic environment where pupils learning English could use this additional language for school learning if the teaching was directed to this end. Her conviction was that *all* teachers should know about language so as to help *all* pupils to develop their full language potential in mainstream classrooms. In Chapter 3 we see her addressing other linguists about the need for distinctive teaching and learning materials, using as a particular illustration those called *Scope, Stage 2*, which she and Hilary Hester had devised for the Schools Council in 1972-74. They had also written a teacher's book to show how special resources could be a model for learning. Amongst their recurrent themes was the conviction that 'the intellectual and emotional side of children's motivation' had to be 'part of the teachers' and writers' concern.'

Chapter 4, written in 1981, was directed particularly to mainstream teachers of English, who were becoming more aware of the potential for learning in the social, cultural and intellectual diversity of their pupils. At the same time they had to confront the prejudices that lurked in multilingual and multicultural education more generally. Josie's work at the Institute of Education encouraged amongst both primary and secondary school teachers greater hospitality to diversity and a wider involvement by them in mainstreaming, partnership teaching and action research over a range of different contexts.

Chapter 3

A Language Learning Materials Analysis: *Scope, Stage 2*

It is worth noting that Scope, Stage 2 *(Schools' Council 1972-74), the only published example of a functional-communicative approach written specifically for use in this country (UK), came out while there was still relative hostility to the approach by those who had accepted and embedded 'withdrawal' from classrooms as the usual practice, but when the expertise in the more dominant structural-situational approach to second language learning was growing. It is also worth noting that the* Scope, Stage 2 *materials were conceived as a* language development *programme, and that they flag at least a conceptual shift (at the time hopefully idealistic in terms of accepted practice) towards the mainstream as the true base for bilingual learners to develop a use of English.*

> *When we started this work, we were looking for a context, for an approach to learning and teaching, and for teaching techniques which would facilitate productive language learning and help to bring the educational performance of learners of English as an additional language closer to their real potential. To meet these demands, for the context and approach we used the subject matter of the school itself and a thematic style of teaching. Into them we incorporated as a natural extension of our earlier work with beginner learners of*

English many of the techniques and practices of second-language teaching. Happily, the children we were aiming at were not generally segregated in special language classes but were in normal classes along with native speakers, a situation of which we wanted to take advantage since we believe that the interests of children at a second stage of learning English as an additional language are best served by following the curriculum of and being a part of a normal class (Levine, 1990, quoted in Teacher's Book, pp. 23-24).

The materials I have chosen in order to test out these socio-linguistic parameters are part of *Scope, Stage 2* (Schools Council, 1972). They are intended for use in Britain with pupils aged 8-13 coming from a variety of backgrounds (eg non-English speaking and/or native English speaking including dialect speakers such as Caribbean) who have diverse educational experience and who, on the whole, underachieve educationally because of language difficulties of one kind or another. The materials based on the study of three themes, *Homes, Travel* and *Water*, consist of the Teacher's Book, which is the core of the scheme, and separate pupils' books and sets of work cards for each theme. I examine the set of materials for the theme *Homes* against the grid to discover, in so far as the grid can tell me, if they encapsulate the use for language in the domain School.

An analysis of some language-learning materials

Homes is one of the three themes which make up the subject matter of *Scope, Stage 2*. There is a pupils' book and a set of work cards and one part of the Teacher's book describes ways of developing the theme, the content of which divides into twelve sections: 'Building', 'Street furniture', 'What are buildings made of?', 'Building a house', 'At home', 'Play', 'Animals and their homes', 'Homes in different areas of the world', 'British architecture', 'Land transport', 'Taking your home with you', 'stately homes'.

Each section subdivides into smaller units. For example, 'At home' contains the following headings: 'Our house', 'Who does these things in your home?', 'Everyone had a job', 'What do you do when you stay in?', 'What do you do when you go out?', 'A visitor', 'Public services', 'My room', 'One busy housewife', 'Inventions'.

Each of the units is made up of Activities, which in turn comprise a number of Steps. It is the level of Activity which is being taken as the unit for analysis.

What the *Scope, Stage 2* materials claim they do

The following quotations are taken from the Introduction to the Teacher's Book.

1. 'The materials aim to assist teachers to develop their pupils' use of English as a tool for learning thinking and communicating ...' (p. 1).

2. 'It is important both for children's language and general development that they are in situations where they must ask questions, discuss and argue, organise, be organised, recount and describe, that they learn to work with each other as well as on their own, and that they have the opportunity to find out things from people, from books and pictures and through other media' (p. 2).

3. '*Scope, Stage 2* encourages language development by presenting the pupils with certain goals which are best achieved by the use of language' (p. 8).

4. '... we are ... concerned with the function of language in their learning and development. We can classify the language skills at which we aim as skills of private language (those skills of comprehension and organisation which may or may not be expressed in speech and writing) and skills of public language (those skills of speech and writing which are directly dependent on previous organisation of thoughts and feelings).

Skills of private language: deducing meaning from contexts, selecting information relevant to particular needs, interpreting selected evidence by establishing contrasts, categories and relationships, organising ideas, feelings, memories, etc, so as to make sense of them for oneself.

Skills of public language: describing accurately, giving precise instructions, making specific enquiries and requests, expressing an opinion citing supporting evidence, expressing ideas, feelings, memories, imaginings so as to make sense of them for others.

Common to both private and public language skills: being able to handle appropriately a variety of styles of both spoken and written language' (p. 13).

5. 'Subject matter ... combined with the activities undertaken ... will determine what the language of the course shall be' (p. 5).

6. 'Although often only one structure is given for a certain function, there may be several alternatives which would meet the needs of the situation equally well. We suggest that you use the structure selected with those who have no way of meeting the linguistic demands of the situation ... On the other hand, native speakers and competent users of the language should not be restricted to the structure given' (p. 9).

Comment on these claims

To quote Halliday again (Halliday, 1968):

Language is a form of culturally determined behaviour and this behaviour includes the ability to take on a range of linguistically defined roles in speech situations. Unless the child grows up in an environment in which all these speech situation roles are open to him, he will fail to master important areas in the grammar of his language. Therefore he must be given the opportunity to behave linguistically in all the culturally determined roles which the language recognises: to ask and answer questions, to give and respond to commands, to explain things, to express reservations, contradictions, contrasts; to vary the key of his utterances; to explore, in other words, a full range of linguistic relations with his interlocutors ... The child has to learn not only to perform in all these roles but also to respond to and identify correctly the roles of others ...

Scope, Stage 2 is concerned with the relationship between language and educational success or failure. That it recognises the importance of the objectives put forward by Halliday is plain (it goes further, not only seeking to provide an environment in which speech situation roles are open to children, but also to offer guidance and systematic teaching in the acquisition of them); but no materials would expect to cover the whole range at one attempt, or even all of one part of it. To attempt to do so would take the emphasis off developing a use of language and put it on knowing about language – something which frequently happens when course writers start with the language first and then look for situations into which to put it.

The materials from *Scope, Stage 2* are written from quite the opposite standpoint. The customary linear progression of language structures is not in evidence. Vocabulary does not follow any word frequency list but is part of the semantic field of the topic in hand. Language items in the Teacher's Book are arranged under the heading 'Language functions and structures' (being those which perform the functions named in a particular case – although pupils are not necessarily restricted to their use). New items are introduced but old ones recur naturally in the context of on-going work.

One would expect analysis by means of the proposed grid to codify much of this information, thus making it possible to say to what extent the materials stand up to their claims.

Homes

- The unit Activity was a workable level to choose to do the analysis since it was able to show the general trends of the materials.

- *Homes* deals overwhelmingly with normative/sanctioned situations. At first glance this might be an expected result for materials which take as their starting point the content of, and the activities undertaken in, the study of school subjects. But since these activities involve people 'living' together and working together, it might be that more consideration should have been given, at this early stage in the course, to some of those unsanctioned activities in which children tend to indulge. Then developing bilinguals and others not able to give as good as they get because of language difficulties could be prepared for the 'battle' (as they are for getting into and working in pairs), rather than having to experience the situation from what one can only assume to be an inferior position.

- In the Introduction to the Teacher's Book for *Scope Stage 2* the following appears:

  > *Homes* pays particular attention to the systematic introduction of the different types of classroom organisation required for theme work of this nature. The early activities require work in pairs. Other kinds of organisation are introduced as the theme progresses (p. 2).

- Because of the deficiencies of the grid it is difficult to comment on the Language Function and Illocutionary Act part of the analysis, except to say that the distribution of language functions is as one might expect and is not inappropriate for the initial stages of a language development course. A further, more delicate analysis is required here.

- Comments about Goodness of Fit have been made above. Worth adding here is the fact that one would expect the fit of the language to the situation to be good, since the writers 'discovered' the language for the course in the content, activities and situations that make up the theme.

- From the point of view of language development for educational purposes (but perhaps not relevant to sociolinguistic parameters?) one important aspect was missing from the grid for analysis – the kinds of listening, speaking, reading and writing skills employed.

Implications for teaching

- Materials organised in the manner of *Homes* provide children with the opportunity of acquiring (in the words of Fishman): 'socio-linguistic communicative-competence with respect to appropriate language usage' in much the same manner of L1 speakers who can be accounted achievers. Which is to say that while involved in content-study, children experience (and are helped to practice) not only in particular modes, roles, tones, etc, but also experience (and practice) changing from one mode, tone, or role, etc, to others.

- I see no reason why First Language materials should not be organised on much the same lines, but with less initial complexity; each step would need to be considered in much greater detail, perhaps at first only taking in one element of role and speech mode and function and gradually building up to a situation that requires changes; some situations which occur naturally in an L1 environment and which *Scope, Stage 2* provides through its organisation, but does not specifically write into the materials, these situations would need to be spelled out in some detail; direct language practice would also need to be provided in a more comprehensive manner.

- The lack of *some* of this detail may well prove to be a deficiency in terms of those teachers who use the materials in Britain. But again it remains to be seen whether teachers from abroad using it require more help situationally, and whether native English speakers need more help with direct language-teaching method than the Teacher's Book Introduction or the method disguised in the page-by-page commentary gives.

- The analysis has indicated some areas where supporting materials might be desirable. For example, the provision of readers and/or film strips which can stand as 'literature' and which are loosely related to the theme but which deal with some of the situations and attitudes not prevalent in the texts.

References

Abbs, B, Candlin, C (1971) 'Teaching Communicative-Competence', unpublished paper, Lancaster University

Bock, P K (1968) 'Social Structure and Language Structure', in Fishman (1968) pp. 212-222

Creber, J W P (1972) *Lost for Words: Language and Educational Failure.* Penguin

Enkvist, N E (1964) 'On Defining Style: An Essay in Applied Linguistics', in Spencer (1964) pp. 3-56

Ervin-Tripp, S M (1964) 'An Analysis of the Interaction of Language, Topic and Listener', in Fishman, ibid, pp. 185-191

Fishman, J, ed (1968) *Readings in the Sociology of Language.* Mouton

Giglioni, P P, ed (1972) *Language and Social Context.* Penguin

Goffman, E (1964) 'The Neglected Situation', in Giglioni (1972) pp. 61-66

Gregory, M (1967) 'Aspects of Varieties Differentiation', *Journal of Linguistics*, Vol. 3, No. 2, pp. 177-198

Halliday, M A K (1 968) 'Language and Experience', *Educational Review*, Vol. 20, No. 2, pp. 95-106

Halliday, M A K (1969) 'Relevant Models of Language', *Education Review*, Vol. 22, No. 1, pp. 26-37

Hymes, D (1964) 'Towards Ethnographies of Communication: The Analysis of Communicative Events', in Giglioni (1972) pp. 21-44

Kirkwood, J M (1973) 'Analysing the Linguistic and Cultural Content of Foreign Language Text-Books – An Application of Variety Theory', *IRAL* 11, pp. 269-385

Pride, J B (1971) *The Social Meaning of Language*, Oxford University Press

Searle, J (1965) 'What is a Speech Act?', in Giglioni (1972) pp. 136-154

Schools Council (1972) *Scope, Stage 2: A Language Development Course,* Longman

Spencer J, ed. (1964) *Linguistics and Style.* Oxford University Press

Spencer, J, Gregory, M (1964) 'An Approach to the Study of Style', in Spencer (1964) pp. 59-105.

Chapter 4

Developing pedagogies for multilingual classes

It is important to recognise that while devising individual strategies for learning support is important, such narrowly individualised support work, often devised by the support teacher on her own, is not really sufficient to facilitate wider learning, nor will such strategies on their own assist bilingual learners in valuing themselves as active participants in classroom life and learning. Individual strategies work best when they are complementary to interactive learning, the integrated use of all the language modes, and the encouragement of bilingual pupils in the use of all *their language knowledge and abilities* (Levine, 1990 p.36).

The teaching of English as an additional language to children in this country, in so far as a tradition is established, has been in the hands of a band of dedicated, specialist teachers who, until quite recently, have worked within a withdrawal system of one kind or another – which one depending on what was regarded as a favourable *administrative* solution to the 'problem' of 'non-English speakers' in 'our' schools.

Throughout this history there has always been a minority view among specialist language teachers that the needs of 'second-language learners' would be served best by being part of a 'normal' class, following the 'normal' curriculum' – given, of course, that the 'normal' class and the 'normal' curriculum in any individual case was actually worth joining. This group of people would say that the difficulty has been to persuade other specialists, administrators and 'ordinary' class and subject teachers that joining in was best.

Over the years a rationale for this has grown – along with that for mixed ability grouping – that goes beyond language learning into the whole development of children: linguistic, cognitive, social, attitudinal: a rationale which does not isolate each of these for separate treatment. (You could say the same, for example, about the teaching of reading, where, if it is taught as if it were possible to learn it as an accretion of separate hierarchically arranged units, learners are deprived of the opportunity of effectively bringing to the task their natural competencies. As a result of undergoing such treatment, they can come to view themselves as being without the skill or wit to learn.)

The argument for 'whole' reading and for mixed ability teaching has been developed outside the teaching of English as an additional Language, but individuals in both groups have been – perhaps unknown to each other – developing in their own ways similar attitudes towards anti-racist teaching and the role of language in learning to the point where both groups could say that the best way to develop skills and fluency in language, the best ways to promote inter-group understandings and sharing of power, is to learn how to do it as one goes along in real life situations (and that includes school) – but with the right kinds of support.

For very good reasons this view is gaining ground both within and without the specialist language teaching lobby. Teachers do not like the racist, anti-social, anti-educational implications of leaving this particular group of learners (those who are developing as bilinguals) to manage as best they can on the periphery of the class. Nor do they like the isolationist implications of withdrawal. So, even while recognising that the past is ever with us ('I wish I could do something to help them but what can one do when there's twenty-eight others in the class?', 'You teach them English then I'll teach in my subject', 'How can they go into ordinary classes and do ordinary curriculum work unless they have a good grounding in vocabulary and structure?') more and more specialist teachers want to work in 'ordinary' classes alongside children doing 'ordinary' work, and 'ordinary' class teachers want to know how to work with developing bilinguals in their classes.

The question being asked then is: 'What do we need to know about additional language learning/subject knowledge/English mother-tongue teaching that will help us teach our subject/class better? Such a question suggests that the intentions of teachers and the needs of their pupils are about to overlap in more fruitful ways than before. More fruitful for the children's learning and language and their social development, and more fruitful in furthering the development of teaching styles that are about the language, social and learning needs of all children.

The solution of withdrawal being no longer the only one we can allow ourselves, the question I want to address is: 'What do I need to know about additional language learning that will help me teach my subject better?' 'What are the tools of hospitality?'

Hospitality to diversity: some general tactics

a. *joining in*

> Let me take a small point first about finding ways of making meaningful what is often only a hollow phrase: being hospitable to diversity. For the children it is the problem of how to get into the discourse, how to fulfil the demands of any particular teacher and subject classroom. In addition, it is also how to take on the ambience of the class he or she has joined. Bilingual speakers who are learning to use English often know what they are required to do, but do not know how to put into words the questions they want to ask or the knowledge that they know they have. The uncertainties and diffidence can permanently damage their ability and willingness to learn and to

join in the community of school. At the very least, they must be able to ask a neighbour what to do. For developing bilinguals and others who are entering a strange environment, such small things can make the difference between feeling welcomed (and, therefore, able to accept the invitation to work together) and feeling rejected. Many of them are bemused by their lack of success in English schools, coming as they may have done from successful school careers elsewhere.

b. *tunes in the head*

In secondary schools, learners of English as an additional language are probably not exposed to enough spoken discourse – including being read to – for them to be able to internalise well enough the tunes and rhythms of English. Even in English lessons, this is probably the case. But if they are to develop their 'own voice', speak, listen, read and write fluently then they must, at least, have as much opportunity to hear the English of others as they are given opportunity to read and write for themselves. Reading to the children takes on new meaning in multilingual classes. It is a most satisfying form of offering literary models.

c. *monitoring learners' devices*

Children often know very well what will help them best in a particular matter. By letting them 'tell' us how to work with them, we enter a mode of learning and teaching which enables us 'to start where the kids are at', rather than do what we often, and so unprofessionally do, make the kids start where we are at.

To write fluently is difficult with limited vocabulary and structures. It is additionally so when you are aware that you are likely to get the grammar of the language wrong. If you are the sort of person who is meticulous about 'getting it right', then you are likely to be paralysed by a writing task. Kun Sung, then a fourth year boy, exactly this meticulous kind of person, taught me how to help others like him at a similar stage in writing in English. The previous year he had had some special English tuition at the local language centre. In addition, because of his English lessons in Hong Kong he was no stranger to exercises of the filling-in-blank variety. He was extremely imaginative about their use. He wrote and left blanks where he did not know what to write or where he was unsure about usage. Then he would say, 'Miss, come and help me.' It was my task – not his – but in consultation with him, to fill in the blanks!

In transforming the exercise, he could be both ambitious about vocabulary and also cautious in those areas where he had uncertainties (in his case, and it will come as no surprise, about verb forms). However, in both ambitious and cautious ways he was helping himself to learn, using what he knew about language skills as they had come to him through his first language (in this case, a sense of fluency), and what he had met as language learning techniques as they had come to him from learning English.

Of course, it doesn't require only an adult to help in this kind of thing. A pupil-colleague could just as easily have collaborated with him. Once the adult understands what kinds of processes are at work, it is easy to hand over some of the responsibility to the children themselves. A balance must be maintained, though, since the new users of English will need to show their teacher how they are getting on.

d.   *support with comprehension*

Certain kinds of understanding can often be promoted by visual clues; for example using film or video recordings where available of plays, novels or short stories being read in class. The children need time to assimilate all the many kinds of details that are coming at them, so another strategy is, as often as possible, to go over again, with those who need it, the content and the assignment – perhaps taking each further back than in the general lesson. (See the section below on task setting.) Encourage the children to ask the questions; help them to frame their responses. Only that way will you get to know what support they need. Only that way will they get practice in construing, considering, testing out their own thoughts, understanding those of other people, and in appropriately expressing it all. Again, show them how to do all this. Because reading round and asking 'comprehension' questions as a check to their understanding of what has been read seems only to make children anxious, once again it is worth encouraging them in initiating collaboration in their learning. Whether reading aloud or reading silently is their own best way of understanding a text, they are bound to encounter vocabulary, phrases and whole chunks of text that they *know* they don't understand. Again, phrases are needed and again, choose phrases that are appropriate for the children's situation. Mine, offered here, are only rough examples of kinds of sentence frames one might employ. 'What does it mean when...' 'What does this word/bit mean?' 'Why does X do Y?' or to a pupil-colleague: 'What do you make of this (bit)?'

Once these interchanges are established, then helpful questioning that can lead young readers into deeper understanding of a text can be seen for what it really is – and not as part of an interrogation, of linguistic competence.

Hospitality to diversity: forethought, afterthought and action

Joining in, tunes in the head, monitoring learners' devices, support with comprehension are examples of the invitational mode in pedagogy, things that one can do then and there out of *ordinary* hospitality. In this section, I want to look, by brief example, at two aspects of our *professional* hospitality: how we make clear to ourselves what the demands of our lessons are and how we might analyse responses to them. The first of these is Task Analysis and the second is Error Analysis. Both of these contribute to the manner in which we achieve a fruitful match between our pupils, ourselves and the materials/content/ methods we work with in our classrooms.

a. *task analysis*

Much work in specialist language teaching focuses on linguistic data directed at vocabulary, structure and function – although the best of it won't begin with the planning of the work at these levels. The authors of *Scope, Stage 2*, (Schools Council, 1972) for instance, planned the materials as if they were planning classroom work where language use was recognised as important for other learning. What they did was:

- choose the topic

- gather the subject matter

- decide appropriate activities and organisations for the learning to take place

- allow to emerge, from the subject matter and activities, the language functions necessary for understanding and exploring the topic

- choose, for the benefit of second-language learners, structures and vocabulary which would enable them to perform the functions

- create material which is core, and other which provides extensive practice of language in use

- suggest ways in which specialist language practice can be provided

- see that there was a range of styles, register and language-linked learning skills demanded of learners, *and also* that they should be supported in their learning of them.

Such support will attend, among other things, to what makes an assignment more or less difficult for an individual, and it will be not only linguistic criteria. Any one of the following may play a part:

- how much is to be done

- how much help is given

- what kind of activity is to be undertaken

- how complex the presentation is to be

- whether new vocabulary items are present

- the nature of the subject content

- structural variety.

The aspect of Task Analysis that I want to highlight is at the level of language-linked learning (eg extracting information from texts, relating text to diagrams) rather than that of language items (eg vocabulary associated with a subject, use of linking words in an extended piece of writing). The rest have to do with fostering communication and commitment among those in the classroom – eminently worth considering after an event for future action.

However, such things as the elements of learning that are language-linked can be analysed prior to the event, and they need to be where multilingual classes are concerned. For many children the instruction 'Get into groups and discuss X' will be enough opportunity to bring their own learning strategies to bear. For more inexperienced others, opportunity only is not enough. They need something more. But do we always know what?

For example, take this common task in English: read a short story/poem, talk about it in small groups, write about it for homework (alternatively, the 'end product' might be to prepare a report of the discussion to present to the rest of the class).

The language linked elements entailed would include:

getting started
reading the text
reading comprehension
reading aloud (possibly)

collecting information

picking out ideas in the text

note taking

forming own ideas and responses however tentatively

matching ideas in the text to own thoughts and experiences

stating all of these, and

stating the relationships made between them

conducting discussion

listening comprehension

expressing own ideas

agreeing with others' opinions and statements

disagreeing

questioning

responding to questions

interrupting

remaining silent

collecting opinions together – if joint report is to be made

listening comprehension

organising strategies appropriate to the nature of the discussion

note taking

preparation for writing – if individual work to be done

musing

organising strategies

taking decisions about the view to be expressed in the writing

reporting back

organising strategies

using notes

speaking extended logical text in an appropriate style for retaining listeners' attention

writing own piece

organising strategies

being prepared to 'accept' new ideas that come by virtue of doing own writing

writing extended logical text in an appropriate style

The list is not ordered entirely hierarchically, although, obviously, some sub-headings must necessarily come before others in the process of performing the task. Also obvious is how many interlinked processes are called into play. Task Analysis, which should never be taken to be suggesting offering pupils less than a whole activity, gives clues to where support might be offered *within* the whole activity.

Linked with this particular type of task is the question of accessibility of a single text to a whole mixed ability group or class. One solution to this is offering specially prepared texts. It is one which is often relevant. Another is to follow Stenhouse and allow to all children what is offered as a right to 'clever' children and advanced students: the opportunity of engaging with something that is too hard for them! University students do this all the time, getting to know their material through engaging in discussions about it.

b. *Error Analysis*

Error Analysis is a technique developed in Applied Linguistics for the observation of second-language learning development. It can apply to both spoken discourse and written text although in its earliest, narrowest formulation it was applied to the omission, addition, selection and ordering of grammatical and lexical items in speech or writing. It is not such an unpromisingly negative a technique as it sounds. A distinction is made between lapses, mistakes and errors. Lapses are slips of the tongue or pen, mistakes are the selection of the wrong style for a particular situation, errors in second-language learners are 'those features of the learner's utterances which differ from those of any native speaker' (Corder, 1973, p.260). None of these are to be regarded as morally reprehensible since everyone makes lapses, and the words 'mistake' and 'error', although here they apply to someone doing something which breaks a rule, it is a rule which is not yet known to them.

A second important point to take on is that additional language learners who do not make many mistakes may be being over-cautious and allowing themselves to do only what they know they can do.

A third point is that some errors will be systematic and others apparently made at random. I was interested to note recently that the English verb forms of a Cantonese speaking boy were wrong but that he had a system, always 'correctly' expressed within itself, of indicating past perfect, present perfect, past and present aspects of verbs. He knew the distinctions, merely had not yet acquired the forms.

Within language we can say that errors and mistakes are caused by lack of experience in the formulation of appropriacy rules of phrases, sentences, discourse; of reference ('brother' for the relationship we would choose to define as 'cousin'); of style ('No miss, you fuck off, you wrong!' for 'I'm really sorry to have to tell you, but it isn't true, what you're saying').

However, one major source of error in language use stems from outside language itself: it can often be traced to the way in which we teach. Consequently, now, when I'm looking at children's work, some of the criteria which I bring to bear in assessing it are extra-linguistic.

- what was the teaching context?

- how much help did the pupil get?

- was the task realistic?

- what thought processes and cultural experiences did they demand?

- to what extent were pupil's and teacher's intentions matching?

- did the pupil have to move more towards the teacher than the teacher made moves towards the pupil?

- is the pupil taking risks?

- is s/he prepared to be adventurous?

- is s/he demonstrating a personal tone of voice?

- is s/he aware of the shaping and patterning of certain literary styles?

- at what point is the pupil in the progress towards full form of expression?

- can one catch the tone, intention and shaping of a piece of work by reading it aloud?

In a practical error analysis session held at a conference on Language in Inner City Schools, in January 1980, the following general points were made. These, taken together with those made above, I want to suggest, are a rich enough set of suggestions, questions and comments to begin thinking about and creating good learning environments for multilingual classes.

– Either directly or indirectly children are using models to work from. Part of what we need to intuit is what these models are. A child writing as s/he speaks may be demonstrating *inexperience* in aspects of written language, but s/he is also demonstrating both initiative (the degree to which s/he is able to risk) and the manner of his/her process of the move towards standard written English.

– We should read children's work from the point of view of their intentions, pick up also their 'tone of voice' otherwise the generative aspect of an error can be missed.

– Evidence of progressive states of inter-language cannot be deduced from one piece of work.

– There is a need to know the setting of a piece of work. Sometimes errors can be induced by the models presented or the direct teaching undertaken.

– There is always a chance that the teacher will assume incorrectly what the learner's intentions are, mistake his or her meanings and therefore make inappropriate corrections. Often they can be nothing more than imposing the teacher's style on the child.

– The quantity and type of correction will vary considerably and depend at least on the individual child's approach to learning and on the distance or closeness of the pupil's relationship with the teacher.

– Wherever possible, negotiation over a child's writing should take place *with* the pupil.

References

Corder, S P (1973) *Introduction to applied linguistics.* Penguin

Richards, Jack (1974) *Error Analysis: perspectives on second language aquisition.* Longman

Schools Council (1972) *Scope, Stage 2: a language development course.* Longman

Stenhouse, L in Ruddick, J. (ed) (1978) *Learning to teach through discussion.* University of East Anglia

Chapter 5

The potential of a language model for the development of the language of bilingual pupils

Modelling appears to be a process by which pupils internalise what to do, and which, at the same time, offers teachers clues to developing teaching practice (Levine, 1990 p.60).

Our starting point has been the *Kingman Report* into the teaching of the English Language, though we are not interested in offering a detailed critique. All we want to ask is 'Why this model?' 'Why this particular selection from all that is known about language?' We see in the model little that can help teachers understand the relationship of knowledge to use, and this mismatch is of particular concern in relationship to the entitlement of bilingual children from minority communities in schools.

We address the needs of bilingual pupils and seek to show how the current framing of the debate on the government side disenfranchises them from their entitlement – as it does implicitly in many other groups of students. We comment on four areas in the report which significantly affect bilingual students: the position of bilingual learners, knowledge about language, attainment targets, and language models, the last of which is an extended section offering an alternative model.

The position of bilingual learners

There is an obvious, broad mismatch between the direction for English teaching proposed by the Kingman Committee with its emphasis on grammatical structure, and the direction teaching English as a second language (ESL) has taken over the past 10-15 years. ESL has moved away from the explicit teaching of language forms and structures, and their trial usage within carefully controlled contexts on the Foreign Language teaching model[1]. The new direction is towards the encouragement and support of developing communicative competence within contexts of use (classrooms in ordinary primary and secondary schools) where bilingual pupils acquire English as an additional language alongside and through the extension of their curricular knowledge, skills and understanding. This is an enterprise that stresses that in learning English bilingual students are widening their functional range beyond and including their use of their other languages[2].

The Swann Committee report, *Education for All* (DES, 1985) recommends the practice of bilingual students, even those at early stages of learning English, receiving education alongside peers of their own ages within the mainstream. Bilingual mainstreaming is already being put into practice in many LEAs, in parallel with the mainstreaming of children with special educational needs as recommended by the Warnock Report (1978), and for somewhat similar reasons: a full and fair curriculum is available only within the mainstream; both sets of pupils – and the small number who fall into both categories – benefit from the intellectual and linguistic stimulus of participation in ordinary schooling; separate provision stigmatises both sets of pupils as educationally inferior and disadvantages them socially when they later rejoin the mainstream. In the case of bilingual students, racism amplifies these disadvantages.

Bilingual pupils should be seen as part of the pupil population whose learning needs are served by the National Curriculum in English, and not as students of some other kind of English. The special circumstances of bilingual pupils (even though they form 30% and more of pupils in some 20 LEAs) have not – with the single exception of Welsh/English speakers

– so far been considered in any of the processes of arriving at the content and assessment schemes for the National Curriculum. And this despite the Kingman Committee's statement on entitlement:

> there is no need to justify, the claim that all children in school are entitled to be helped to achieve the highest possible levels of linguistic competence (my emphasis) and understanding ... (DES, 1988, p 49)

Knowledge about language

The Kingman Committee Report proposes a model of language for teachers (especially English teachers) and two sets of attainment targets for pupils – explicit knowledge about language and competence that is implicit, but will be demonstrated in use, and it is this second aspect of language knowledge that public and therefore comparative assessment will focus on.

Language knowledge for teachers

Primary and secondary teachers across the board are directed to take on the knowledge proposed in the Kingman Report (recommendations 8-17). We have major reservations about the kind of knowledge proposed (see Language Models section of this chapter).

The phrase 'knowledge about language' is often used in the report as though it were synonymous only with knowledge about the English language. We deplore the parochial emphasis on English – and on a too circumscribed notion of Standard English, at that – as though this exists independently of any other languages, literature or cultures. People learning English as an additional language bring to that task the knowledge of their first language (and literature), and teachers need to find ways of bringing this knowledge into the classroom.

However, we still see some benefits deriving from a renewed focus on knowledge about language in teacher education – benefits for all pupils but perhaps particularly for the education of bilingual pupils in schools. Even if the Kingman model were adopted for this teacher education, our experience of teachers' learning is that it regularly transcends the prescribed limits of their courses and in-service training sessions.

Knowledge about language for students

The report separates language in use from explicit language knowledge, but the committee seems unclear about the precise role knowledge about language is to play for the teaching and learning of English. At some points the claim for knowledge of grammatical terms and functions is made largely in relation to its power in enabling pupil and teacher to reflect together on the pupil's use of language in speech, in writing and in critical approaches to literature. At other points it puts forward a stronger claim for teaching about language – that this will lead to improvements in language use. There are unexamined assumptions in the report about how teachers can and should teach pupils to produce written standard (possibly even spoken) English in accordance with learnt rule systems. An example is the Committee's solution to the large pedagogical problems implied by the difficulties young writers meet in coming to use deixis appropriately. Paragraph 29, p.13 blandly assures teachers that all they have to do is teach a general rule of reference. This is a ludicrous suggestion, failing as it does to acknowledge well known analyses of the psychological processes involved for young children in 'disembedding' language from immediate contexts such usages imply.

The explicit position of the Kingman Committee is that assessing the language pupils can already operate shows best their (tacit) knowledge about language, while explicit language knowledge helps pupils to talk about what they already know and can do (and which can safely be left to teachers to assess). Why then does the report smuggle in directions to teachers to overtly teach systems whose best use is to generalise and reflect on aspects of the complex multi-stratal, multi-functional systems that is language in use?

When watching their pupils acquiring English as an additional language, teachers who are not specialist language teachers have been surprised by the relative speed of acquisition, and by the integrated nature of the learning. They have seen their pupils – after a shorter or longer period of listening in – acquiring the complex, interrelated parts of the language system of English as one integrated operation, so that intonation, stress, discourse strategies, interactive rules, comprehension and oral responses of increasing complexity develop together. Misguided attempts to introduce pupils to rule systems, for example of syntax or pronunciation, interfere with the less conscious process of language learning and tend to cause rather than correct 'non-native' errors.

Pupils in the process of learning English seem to benefit most from internalising the typical rhythms and cadences of different kinds of discourse – conversations they hear and join in with, stories told and read to them and, gradually, more formal exposition.

Another notable feature of additional language acquisition in communicative situations that contrasts with the form of the model presented in the Kingman Report is that pupils take on and reproduce features of the larger units of discourse (story forms, conversations, sets of instructions, sequences of events and processes) before they give their attention to detail of lexical, syntactic and phonological correctness.

Explicit language knowledge is useful to students of an additional language largely as a way of reviewing parts of the language system they have already learnt to control, and for sorting out relationships between different parts of the system. Increasingly, later, as these students become more conscious and deliberate about their intention in writing and in spoken interaction, they will need to use different kinds of metalanguage in discussions with their teacher and in their own self-assessment. In pupil profiling and assessment, teachers see for themselves the need to introduce students to terminology and concepts about language in ways the Kingman Committee appears entirely to overlook.

Attainment Targets

If these observations about the processes of additional language acquisition are well founded (see, for example, Dulay, Burt and Krashen) then they raise doubts about the validity of target knowledge identified at the different attainment levels for second bilingual learners – and, more generally for all pupils. The committee's failure to relate recent research in cognitive psychology and in education on the development aspects of speaking, listening, reading and writing to their account of the linguistic understandings children need at different ages causes them to set up arbitrary 'stages' in the development on 'English'. Attainment needs to be related to experience and access, and not just to age.

The most harmful effect on bilingual learners lies in the official decisions about examining and assessment procedures, to treat language as though it were the same order of knowledge as that in the other curriculum areas. The result: equating language with English, and treating it as though all pupils' experience of language is the same and therefore easily measurable, will be seriously to underestimate the ability of pupils who know a different first language.

Pupils whose first language is not English, especially those arriving in Britain during the course of their schooling, have always been severely disadvantaged by the fact that at 16+ the entire cohort is tested by public examinations on whose outcome future life chances are almost entirely dependent. A significant number of very successful students, especially in Science, Maths and Technology, have come from amongst those whose first language (and initial education) is not English. Will tests designed to discriminate their precise knowledge and use of English at these various stages lead to the provision of additional resources to support their learning? Or is it more likely that low scores in the 'language' area will lead to pupils' exclusion from courses or colleges that could lead to their academic success – and have in the past led to such success? What price then, the entitlement to achievement, and to participatory rights in a democracy? This group of students often makes very clear the parochial and discriminatory aspects of British educational thinking, the effects of which are not limited to second language learners.

Language models

The English curriculum must be broad if it is to provide opportunities for pupils to develop productive and receptive skills in speech and writing, if it is to make full use of all their experience of literature and critical approaches to text, if pupils are to develop knowledge about language that is useful. This applies to all students whether they have English as a first or an additional language. Indeed, because English teachers have a broad curriculum, and therefore a broad model of language in mind, they have increasingly been able to respond to the learning needs of black and bilingual pupils. The language model proposed in this chapter targets the knowledge and understandings implied by just such a broad approach.

It is clear that a model must work for those that have to or need to use it; it is equally clear that to be useful, a model must represent well the reality it seeks to capture. But reality is frequently too complex and we are left with choices: we can choose to treat only those portions that we understand as if they were the whole; or we can sketch that whole again, in so far as we perceive it. Characteristic of a model is that it is often most useful, and certainly best understood, by the person who constructed it as an explanatory tool. A model is bound by the theories, precepts and practices (whether inspected or naturalised) of the discipline from which it springs. Thus, it does not necessarily travel well – either from person to person within a discipline or across disciplines. A model which is imported into or exported out of another discipline has to be seen as a possible contribution to any question posed in its new sphere of potential influence. Little consideration has been given to this basic fact of practical theory making. A model is designed to inform, to promote discussion not uncritical acceptance, to bear possible transformation – even rejection – if it cannot respond to the questions being asked of it. Examined in the light of these criteria, Kingman's proposals are found wanting. They are reductive, as are the terms of reference and the supplementary guidance to the Curriculum Group on English.

In this section, we sketch a model for the teaching and learning of English as an additional language which can help teachers in mainstream

71

classrooms and those concerned with supporting learning in relation to mainstream curriculum. Our concern is to:

- to create a rich climate for learning and development
- to know and understand the features of that climate
- to be able to derive a language curriculum from it
- to be able to assess their students' progress in relation to it.

Our model is a pedagogic one and it relates to bilingual students and their acquisition and development of a use of English.

The phrase 'acquisition and development' is used here in the broadest possible sense to mean:

- to learn to understand, speak, read and write in a new language
- to grow into the possession of a wide sociolinguistic repertoire that includes registers of English and the use of languages other than English; that is, be able to function in a wide variety of situations and cultural contexts, including, of course, the domain School
- to gain insight into and, increasingly, conscious control over their own processes of thinking, learning and studying, and of the role of language in these processes
- to develop skills of critical analysis
- to learn to reflect on many of these tacitly learned skills and processes in order, increasingly, to hold some formalised knowledge both about language systems and about how language and languages work, and relate to each other, in society.

The term 'pedagogic' is used to link the environmental requirements we have mentioned with several other teacherly needs, namely:

- to have a working model of language in use in our classrooms
- to have a breadth and depth conceptualisation of what constitutes language

- to take meaning and function in language as central to our understandings about it and its systems – including its grammatical systems.

that is, to link the environmental requirements with our need for a generative model that will help us teach developmentally.

The model of language offered by Kingman is trivial, partial and unmotivated towards pedagogy and the processes of learning. It stands up to none of the requirements of usefulness nor offers any of the kinds of knowledge about language and learning outlined here. If bilingual students are to develop a use of English that enables achievement in our system (which, we should not have to remind ourselves, is their system, too), then we must, at one and the same time, take what we have described as acquisition and development to be the language entitlement they share with all other learners in schools and grant the same status to their bilingualism as that granted to their bilingual counterparts in Wales (who currently are the only linguistic group in the country to be granted such official recognition). We have done badly in offering this respect to date – as this young graduate teacher testifies in writing about her own experience[3]. Speaking of a recent educational experience, she says:

... it was a totally new experience for me to have (my culture) viewed legitimately in the classroom. I was not seen as just black nor was I seen as just a victim of racism but I actually had a language, literature and culture of my own that was important enough to pass on. I found it a very strange experience indeed to be in a classroom situation where the ideas that were being expressed on identity, language and culture reflected my feelings and ideas on the subject. I became conscious for the first time of how much I was forced to divide my life up into two compartments when I had been at school because there seemed to be no common meeting point and I realised (both) how important the relationship between education and one's own experience is (if one is) to derive true benefit from education especially if one is to develop and grow as a human being – and (also) how (the split) affects one's capacity to get the most out of education in its broadest sense.

We should remember, too, that access to this language entitlement, as well as English language entitlement, is gained across a whole school curriculum and not only via the subject English, (although there is no doubt of the distinctive role that can be played by the latter). As a consequence, access to understandings about language-and-learning, language-learning and language-development is therefore the entitlement of all teachers and not only those who teach the subject English.

To the model then.

Of course, we cannot develop it here in full, so, since we are attending to some questions of match and mismatch and have tried to show how the model of language represented by the lists in Kingman so seriously fails to meet the needs of bilingual students developing a use of English and of their teachers, we will develop a way of thinking about language which starts in a not dissimilar place – with the patterns of English grammar.[4] Later, we will turn the whole procedure round, for until that is done, what are interesting facts about language cannot be transformed into a pedagogic model of language.

This is not a modern version of such patterns. It was presented to students on a TEFL diploma course in the mid-sixties – a summary of our study of such patterns for the purpose of teaching English as a Foreign Language. There are surely more adequate models of this kind of knowledge available today than this one, but it is interesting, nevertheless, and already tells us more than the Kingman model, despite its narrow focus, for it has some, if not enough, explanatory power. And that power lies in the fact that it is motivated towards stating meaning relationships – those meanings that are expressed grammatically. This is not just a string of observations, the reasons for knowing them seemingly random. It is a hint that language is systematically organised to codify meaning and that because some meanings are carried in the grammar they do not then have to be stated in any other way (although, of course, they can be and we can choose to do so). Admittedly, such knowledge is not as helpful as a base for our teaching as linguists would like to think it is – the case for moving down to this rather than up from it is surely made – but I would suggest that such a model – although a better one than this – could give people a fair start for recognising what all students, including bilingual students developing a use of English, have learned to do and are approximating towards in relation to patterns of English grammar, would help teachers to pick out what they might overtly want to discuss with a student about grammatical patterning, and would help them make formative assessments about what opportunities for access to language in use they need to make available.

Knowledge about language has grown a-plenty, and it is now easy to see how tiny an area is filled by the grammatical patterns model. The next model[5], also elderly, although younger than the first, shows this. The patterns of grammar of the first model are to be found as a section of **how to say** – which is itself only a part of the whole.

This is a model of communicative competence and it starts in the only possible place – with meaning. This meaning is both what individuals make for themselves and that which comes to them. The model moves to what they have implicitly to know and have in order to do things with and in language. The fact of this being implicit knowledge is expressed in the model by commas, they '**know**' and '**have**'.

Reading the model for producing language, we can say that communicative competence derives from meaning – we have to have the **what to say** – and is linked to comprehension and production of the **do** and **show** by what we **know** add **have**; that is **rule** systems (grammatical, lexical, semantic and communicative) on the one hand, and phonological and written systems on the other. The phonological and written systems – the '**have**' – are distinguished from the others – the '**know**' because they are seen as a different set of phenomena: they are the actual means by which both the '**mean**' and the '**know**' are made manifest. The terms *private language* and *public language* signal that communicative competence needs to be seen as inner speech in the Vygotskian sense (Vygotsky, 1962) as well as language used in interactions.

Unlike Kingman's, this model does not deal only with surface levels. Rather it demonstrates how meanings get encoded in text (spoken and written) and other language-linked behaviour, and when reversed, how text and other language-linked behaviour is understood.

It is, however, one thing to model competence and performance this way: another to specify in any detail how these systems are built. In a language model of what teachers need to know about language, there is a further necessary level of knowledge. It is the level of language function[6]. In model making terms this is a level of list making. Not random lists, but those language functions which arise out of contexts: situational and cultural. It will be useful to make 'job description' specifications of tasks pupils are set, specifications of stages pupils go through in doing tasks, mapping what happens as pupils do tasks, and making descriptions of the contexts in which they do them[7]. There is, currently, a very real attempt to map what is on offer, as evidenced by a great many of the papers edited by Jones and West (1988): *Learning me your language*, but little evidence yet that map makers have understood the need to take a language function approach to delineate the language curriculum. However, if we are to truly know what we are offering in the language curriculum in our classrooms and to understand how language is learned in context, we need to be able to analyse tasks and texts (including literary texts) and to interpret interaction at this function level.

The following list is an example of unpacking a task in language function terms. It should be obvious how important this is in providing for and understanding bilingual pupils' progress. We do not so much need attainment targets to tell us what is to be learned (but which leave us to think up situations and tasks which might teach them). Rather, we need the knowledge that will enable us to see to what degree our pupils can carry out the task set and to what degree our tasks grant access to learning across the broad curriculum that primary teachers and teachers of English would wish to establish. A functional approach is a direct aid to this. As we see it, this functional level is the pivot between broad and narrow knowledge about language, and to be able to analyse tasks and be able to interpret social interaction is the key to a rigorous, consciously held understanding of the curriculum offer in terms of all the aspects of language – including literature.

DISCUSSING A TEXT AND MAKING A REPORT
Collecting Information
reading the text

reading with comprehension

picking out ideas in the text

note taking

matching ideas in the text to own thoughts and experiences

stating the relationships made

Conducting Discussion
listening comprehension

expressing own ideas

agreeing with others, opinions

disagreeing

questioning

responding to questions

Interpreting

interrupting,

Collecting Opinions Together
listening comprehension

note taking

organising strategies

Reporting
organising strategies

reference

production (spoken or written of extended text)

As there is no overall one to one relationship between the forms of structural patterns of language and the functions of language (the grammar occurs over and over again whatever the situation). There is no absolute one-to-one relationship between functions of language and the educational tasks which pupils are set for purposes of their learning. Of course, certain tasks and social groupings have characteristic functions, just as it is open for us to choose particular forms and structural patterns for the performance of functions. It is these dualities that allow pupils to develop their language repertoires through communicative approaches to learning, and why it is so important pedagogically for teachers to think through their curriculum offer from the largest units down rather than the smallest units upwards. Making sense of things comes from perceiving overall coherence.

Our model for language knowledge for teachers would, therefore, start with a mapping of a whole learning activity, deconstructing it into its progressively smaller units, that is, working in the opposite direction from that in which we have presented the parts of our model in this paper.

This final sketch is of an overall activity. It is of language in use in an interactive/social situation which is task-related. The activity was dissecting flowers – secondary Biology or primary Science. The whole activity is taken to comprise the task and what the participants bring to it. Thus, the curriculum offer is set by the teacher and enhanced by the knowledge, experience and language repertoires brought to it by the students. Students gained new knowledge and experience and developed their existing knowledge both in relation to subject content and the learning and/or the further development of experience in language use.

It is the interactions carried out in classrooms and delineated in this sketch that provide the motivating force for students extending and developing their use of spoken and written language. By choosing the particular section that they did from knowledge about language for their model and, therefore, ignoring the things we have spoken about here, the Kingman Report acts to downgrade both this kind of knowledge about language and, implicitly, this kind of teaching. Yet, all students will suffer in their language development and in their educational achievement (including their knowledge about language), none more so than bilingual children developing a use of English, by this exclusion.

We have posed this model as a model of what teachers need to know about language and language in use. There is but one more point to be made: to indicate that this is a guidance model, one that delineates important areas of knowledge relating to the establishment of environments for developing competence in students and to teachers assessing their progress. Hence a pedagogic model. It is not, however, intended as a model from which to teach directly in classrooms, even while it might act as such in the education of teachers.

Notes

1. ESL teaching originally used pedagogies informed by behavoural psychology and by earlier and narrower models of the grammatical structure of language, including those derived from early Applied Linguistics.

2. Later and more sophisticated work by sociolinguists and socially oriented linguists like Halliday emphasised the power of social contexts for language use in enabling meanings to be both generated and encoded and to be understood. Language development in both the language acquired first and in the later acquisition of other languages is analysed as a process of exchanging meaning in social groups and discovering the way language functions are performed. It arises as well from the perceived needs of learners to be free to bring all their linguistic resources to their learning.

3. Shahida Khan, 'Considerations on the Urdu Language: Past and Future', unpublished PGCE course essay, Institute of Education University of London, 1988.

4. From a lecture given by P. Hill on Diploma in Teaching English as a Foreign Language, University of London Institute of Education, 1966-67.

5. From Josie Levine, 'Creating Environments for Developing Communicative Competence', unpublished dissertation for MA in Linguistics for English Language Teaching, University of Lancaster, 1972.

6. The term language function is taken from Halliday and is used here to mean language linked activities and skills; what can be done in and with language; what language functions as.

7. See chapter 4.

References

DES (1985) *Education for All.* (Swann Report). HMSO

DES (1988) *Report for the committee of Enquiry into the Teaching of the English Language* (The Kingman Report). HMSO

Dulay, H, Burt, M, Krashen, S (1982) *Language Two.* Oxford University Press

Jones, M and West, A (eds) (1988) *Learning me your language.* Mary Glasgow and Baker

Vygotsky, L S (1962, 1988 2nd ed) *Thought and Language.* Cambridge MA, Massachusetts Institute of Technology

Chapter 6

'Going back' to the mainstream

The situation as we entered the 1980s, then, was one in which the theories about language and learning which underpinned good mixed ability practice in the mainstream were not yet well understood.

Mainstreaming is a move away from the established practice of withdrawing bilingual pupils from the mainstream curriculum – a practice which negatively affected their status and achievement in schools. Institutionally, mainstreaming is a move away from bilingual pupils being seen chiefly as the responsibility of specialist language teachers, to the view of all teachers having responsibility for them. In language learning terms, mainstreaming for bilingual learners is a move away from disabling monolingual notions that a person must have considerable facility in a language before using it for school learning, and that new language learning, is hindered by the 'interference' of a first, more familiar language (Levine, 1990 pp.26, 29).

(The essay which forms this chapter was written in the summer of 1983. It is thus one of the early versions of this argument, which is continued in the next section. Ed).

The debate about how best to support second language learners in both their learning and their language learning comes to us as a debate about whether or not to withdraw the learners from the mainstream of schooling.

It is a curious issue for us to maintain as central, since all that is currently known about the processes of language development, of learning itself, of the relationship between language and learning, of the growth of intergroup understandings, tells us that developing bilinguals, like all other school students, should be following the mainstream curriculum in mixed ability classes where talk and interaction are central to the learning and teaching that goes on.[1]

The need for a strong form of withdrawal has been argued on the grounds that the conditions which have just been sketched are rarely found, that most mainstream classrooms are experienced by second language learners as places of incomprehension and racism. What this argument slides over, however, is the fact that special language classes can be equally poor places of learning: neither the children nor the teachers have access to a wide enough curriculum, socially the children are ghettoised, and the specialist provision (with honourable exceptions) is too much based in the teaching of linguistic structures in isolation from the natural contexts in which they occur. (This was once standard practice in foreign language teaching.)

When lessons are well learned people get to know quite a lot *about* the language they are learning but usually only learn to use it when they have the opportunity to be in the country where that language is spoken and to interact with native speakers of the language. Plainly, in situations like ours, where the language being learned and its skills have to be put to immediate, even simultaneous use, for both social and educational purposes, such a teaching method is not appropriate. We have seen that if youngsters in this country are to do themselves justice in school, the best language learning will take place when we can arrange for them to learn and practise the language they are learning in communication and interaction with other speakers of that language as they engage on the subject matter of school, ie in real contexts in which the language is used.

Furthermore, where they can do this without being barred from use of their mother tongues.[2]

The pro-withdrawal argument fails to articulate two other education-linked issues: first, the means by which we organise our teaching and, second, the strategies we adopt for teaching.

At one time, withdrawal provision seemed right because it fitted so well with the remedial organisation already in existence. But it further went unchallenged because it fitted so well with both the need of mainstream teachers 'to get on with their normal work' (how could they when there were people in the class who couldn't speak English?) and with language-structure teaching strategies (these being different work from normal teaching). There was no question of devising organisational strategies and a pedagogy from observations and understanding of learners' needs and processes. Teachers' needs were the priority.

In other words, questions about racism, about access to the curriculum, about what motivates organisation in schools, even about language learning, all of which hang over what is available in specialist withdrawal provision are at least as serious as those which threaten the uncaring mainstream class. Most serious is the fact that, even if all withdrawal provision teaching caught up with the best practice which has been developed within it, it would still not fulfil children's learning and language learning needs. Even if it all became, overnight, *communicatively* based and attended centrally to the content of the curriculum, and every language teacher was capable of staging accessible learning tasks which brought the learner close to the conditions for natural language learning, withdrawal would still remain an instrument of isolation. No one teacher can 'do' the whole curriculum. The children still have to 'go back' to the mainstream. The special class protects them from (rather than helps them to cope with) the complexities of society as they are mirrored in the community of the school.

For these reasons, specialist language teachers with a communicative approach to language learning, mainstream teachers who are developing an anti-racist, anti-sexist and class-conscious education, mainstream teachers who are committed to and experienced in the practice of mixed ability teaching and work with the need for all learners, for example, to talk their way to understanding – all agree that second language learners should be in the mainstream. Other mainstream teachers, often less explicit about the issues of race, gender and class and often less aware of the role of language in learning are moving the same way. They want to know how to teach their subjects better. They may have once believed that the children should learn the language first, before joining the mainstream class, and that when they did know enough English they would easily be able to take part in ordinary schooling. But not any more. They have seen the results, both for themselves and for the children, of leaving them unattended on the edges of their classes, and do not like being party to creating failure.

Of course, like every mainstream teacher, they do not have to argue for bilingual learners being in their classrooms. They are already there. (What is conveniently forgotten when support is lent to off-site withdrawal is that it is either part-time or very short term, or both.) The fact is that bilingual learners have never *not* been in mainstream classes – it is only as if that had been so. What is central in the debate is not whether or not to withdraw but how far teachers will be able to accept and then engineer the changes necessary to make classrooms better learning environments for everyone. Mixed ability? Bilingual? Talk as a central learning mode? How far, too, will teachers be able to collaborate? How far will they be able to understand each other's very different starting points? How far will they be able to work their ways towards each other's experience? For despite the innovatory nature of this work, the experience is there to learn from.

These are questions we should ask of everyone, but because they have been given a crucial role to play in initiating the changes, specialist language teachers must make sure they are included among the teachers of whom these questions are asked. Theirs is a full, responsible and necessary task requiring diplomacy and tact. It is absolutely vital that because of their special role they do not collude with circumstance to reinforce the idea that all the wisdom about how to make the responses (even all the wisdom about language and language demands in the school) rests within the tradition of this single specialism. If they do, they will be trapped again in the impossible expectation of trying to do by themselves something which intrinsically cannot be done by one set of people.

Mixed ability, multilingual, multicultural mainstream classrooms (with given and negotiated curricula) are very complex places. There is expertise and knowledge at work within them that are crucial to creating the pro-learning environment we are talking about.

The language specialist's expertise is needed. So is content knowledge of subjects and an understanding of how to set challenging and yet accessible assignments that leave space for learners to develop their own ways of thinking and talking about topics and expressing their own views, that encourage interaction with people as well as engagement with texts.

Few teachers at present know all this from within their own experience, that is why the nature of teacher collaboration is central to success in learning to support second language learners in mainstream classes. The agenda for cooperation is yet to be fully negotiated. It will develop slowly, be as much about teachers learning to work together and respect each other as about children learning to do so, as much about organising classrooms as about designing assignments. And it involves risk.

References

1.   Barnes, D (1976) From *Communication to Curriculum*, Penguin

Barnes and Todd (1977) *Communication and Learning in Small Groups*, Routledge and Kegan Paul

Department of Education and Science (1979) *Aspects of Secondary Education in England and Wales*, Chapter 6 'Language', HMSO

Martin, N, *et al,* (1976) *Writing and Learning*, Ward Lock

Mercer, N (1981) *Language in School and Community*, Arnold

Wells, G (1981) *Learning Through Interaction*, Cambridge University Press

2.   Brumfitt, C J and Johnson, K (1979) *The Communicative Approach in Language Teaching*, Oxford University Press

Dulay, H and Burt, M (1976) 'You Can't Learn without Goofing' in Richards, J: Error *Analysis – Perspectives on Second Language Acquisition*, Longman

Krashen, S (1982) *Principles and Practice in Second Language Acquisition*, Pergamon

Dulay, H, Burt, M, and Krashen, S (1982) *Language Two*, Oxford University Press

WAYS AHEAD

As their experiences of the learning of bilingual children increased, teachers in both primary and secondary schools began to notice a number of changes in their approaches. They could recognise themselves as professionally expert. By the end of the eighties, the notion that bilingual learners make most progress in mainstream classrooms was supported by evidence from other countries. Confluent ideas current in other matters that touched the social nature of language, gender studies for example, were being considered in the context of school learning. As teachers' confidence in 'mainstreaming' grew, Josie Levine wanted a description of 'teaching' that would encompass all the strands of her distinctive practice, a complex of actions and meanings to replace the military metaphors of training and the psychological simplicities of transmission. She describes the central construct of her activities as 'pedagogy'.

The papers which compose this section show the emergence of a new professionalism, formed and fired by a generation of teachers determined to create the conditions necessary for bilinguals to have access to the whole curriculum in terms of their lived experience and their hopes for their future. As reader-students of these pieces we are to become 'conscious and deliberate' in what we do and understand. It is not surprising therefore, that the emphasis on the social nature of these activities is underlined by Vygotsky, whose *parrainage*, a special kind of godparentliness, is at the heart of the more recent essays. Here we also discover that the benefits of knowing more than one language include our gaining the structures of feeling associated with each.

Chapter 7

A new professional mode

The most fruitful partnerships will facilitate appropriate and easeful moves between different combinations of:

- *both teachers working with a whole class, groups, or individuals;*

- *teachers changing role, eg, as lead or support teacher;*

- *consultation over the choice of materials, tasks and processes to be employed.*

Working out partnerships is not simply a matter of attending to the issues already indicated. There is also the all important matter of the process of partnership teaching development itself to be considered. Even the best intentioned partners throw up problems and difficulties for each other. Teachers consciously engaged in creating pedagogy and curriculum development for a particular classroom need also to have a conscious interest in considering the appropriate means of developing their professional working relationship (Levine, 1990 p.32).

Collaborative teaching, or as I would prefer to call it, cooperative teaching, is a form of team teaching. As a means of making school learning more effective, it has a history as an idea. It is important to look at this history and how various forms of team teaching have been argued for and regarded, otherwise in our advocacy of cooperative teaching we could find ourselves lamely putting old cases as if they were new, or worse, we could fail to express the central virtue of cooperative teaching; namely, its potential for powering our professional development.

At the simplest level something we can call team teaching offers within one subject area a division of labour to the teaching team and an opportunity for the students to hear more than one voice. At a more theorised level, team teaching integrates certain parts of the curriculum. The rationale and the pragmatics are somewhat different, when the team doing the teaching is drawn from different subject areas; people of equal curriculum status within a school agree, by their participation, to become generalists but maintain their specialism within that. Teachers participating in this work are likely to have their own teaching groups. The team work is done in lead lessons which all groups attend, in the drawing up of the syllabuses and the marking and sharing of materials. In good circumstances, there is a division of labour when the opportunity is taken to have (say) five teachers for four classes, so that teaching groups may be smaller. Thus individual teachers have fewer students to attend to and individual students have more teacher time available to them.

The decision may be taken to have larger groups than the separate classes with the extra teacher shared out amongst them. Sometimes it is possible for all the teachers concerned to be timetabled in support as well as class teacher roles. This sharing is welcomed. In practice, it means the teacher gets some rest from full responsibility of class organisation and the sustaining of its work.

A third kind of team teaching is the participation of a remedial teacher or specialist language teacher in a mainstream subject class or group as a support for certain students perceived as having learning difficulties of one kind or another. Teachers participating in this form of team teaching have differential status in curriculum terms. The role of the support teacher is then to follow the lead of the mainstream teacher and to interpret the lesson for those who are having difficulty with it in its primary form. On the surface, this appears to be the same as the support role referred to in relation to the teaching of cross-curricular studies. The psychological structure is, however, very different. Support teachers have their own expertise, but this is all too frequently disregarded if they appear not to know enough about the specialism displayed by the teacher they are supporting. Yet in this, as in other forms of team teaching, individual students benefit from increases of adult attention.

Why then, despite these well intended outcomes, do we find that team teaching does not seem to be enjoyed by the majority of teachers? Why do so many teachers' hearts sink at the thought of engaging in it? Why do so many say it won't work? In the simplistic form of team teaching given as my first instance in which division of labour is seen as the prime factor, the teachers concerned may be required to relate to one another only because lessons in a subject are split between them. Nevertheless, I have include this pattern because the implication of their dual responsibility is that they will need to consult each other about their work. This is the central issue, not only for those teachers, but for all teachers engaged in all forms of curriculum liaison.

Where is the time to come from for the necessary liaising to take place? Time for consultation, discussion, reviewing of their team work, disputing and negotiating of inevitable difficulties – is so rare as to be remarkable. It is this almost systematic lack of provision, made worse by current government policy which results in the cutting of resources and staff, that is the root cause of an understandable resistance in most teachers to undertake work which has a built-in potential, only too often fulfilled, for dissatisfaction.

Collaborative teaching within a single subject area is more straightforward than in cross-curricular integrations, where teachers sometimes think that their students are short-changed by not getting enough of what their teachers want them to learn. Other teachers, just as keen on learning but with a different approach, are anxious not to revert to transmission modes of teaching. The result is that, instead of being a broadening experience for students over a range of learning styles and different kinds of materials, integrated lessons may have, again, the transmission· of teaching 'stuff' and too narrow a range of language-linked activities.

When teachers work together in the same classroom – whether with integrated curricula or not – variations on these themes seem to be endless. 'How can I work with the students I'm supposed to help when all we get is an exposition from the front?', 'Some of the lessons are so formal I don't see how anyone learns let alone the kids learning English', or alternatively, 'Some of the lessons are so informal I can't prepare anything to help the bilingual kids', 'They don't want me in', are some of the variations from disenchanted specialist language support teachers. Mainstream teachers often express sentiments like these: 'All she wants to do is make something called, 'sentence patterns out of lessons", 'I'm committed to having all the kids in, but the ESL teacher doesn't really want to do it', 'These support teachers expect me to do all the controlling and the marking while they just sit back and teach one or two. It's not fair.'

When attempted classroom liaisons are characterised by comments like these, the participants are not experiencing or engaging in anything one can call cooperative teaching. What are the differences then? What is it that has caused a growing minority of teachers to want to engage in it, some LEAs to adopt it as policy and Swann (Department of Education and Science, 1985) to recommend it as one of the ways of achieving 'education for all'? Not necessarily the ways in which the teachers organise their team teaching – for cooperative teaching may take the form of, or move in and out of, any one of the kinds of team teaching I earlier sketched. Not necessarily the experiences they undergo, for participants in cooperative teaching may face any or all of the difficulties I also touched upon earlier – including arguing considerably about particular issues. Not in fact that it is easier to do than others, for it is not. The same structural and personal obstacles are still met. The differences seem to be: whether or not the participants expect difficulties as part of the process they must attempt to negotiate; whether or not they are prepared to move pragmatically towards building trust in each other so that they develop equality in analysing classroom events; whether or not they see themselves as researchers jointly engaged in creating a pedagogy for a particular classroom at a particular time, for cooperative teaching touches as much on teachers' learning about and developing a dynamic curriculum as it is a strategy for supporting student's learning; and all of these are interconnected features of a move towards a social and academic curriculum based on discussion, research and analysis. It is a new professional mode.

Reference

Department of Education and Science (1985) *Education for All* (The Swann Report). HMSO

Chapter 8

Pedagogy: the case of the missing concept

The intellectual commitment of the teachers, their creativity and willingness to learn from the on-going events of their classrooms, the way in which they themselves are in an observing and learning mode about how to establish and improve this interactive teaching and learning context becomes obvious when we consider the fact that classrooms which are merely nominally designated mixed ability, multicultural, multilingual, do not deliver the fair curriculum and opportunities for language and learning that we seek. Classrooms do not become productively interactive simply by virtue of telling children to talk to each other. They are not socially harmonious across culture, race and gender simply because children of different social class, ethnicity and sex are grouped together. Mixed ability teaching does not happen just because there is mixed ability grouping. The learning of English as a second language does not take place in effective ways just because there are pupils in the classes who have need of this facility. Nor is a classroom multilingual simply because there are children in it who know languages other than English or dialects other then standard – they are certainly not so if in them students feel constrained or even ashamed about the use of their language and dialects.

The development of successful practice stems fundamentally from accepting the diversity which is represented in these classrooms as a constructive base for curriculum development, and rigorously addressing challenge of classroom reality (Levine, 1990 p.286).

Many years ago, when I was looking for a concept-framing word to stand for what I like to think of as the greatest of the plastic arts: the on-going practice of teaching, I decided to ignore its negative connotations and adopt the word 'pedagogy' into my professional vocabulary.

I was looking for a word which I could use in my work in teacher-training and which, with some appropriate explanation, would stand for that complex of thinking, feeling, information, knowledge, theory, experience, wisdom and creativity which are the inherent, acquired and continuously-honed qualities of individual good teachers. I needed also a word, the same word if possible, to carry within it the sense of teaching as a theorising profession offering scope for the building of theory and practice out of its essential elements via processes of reflection, analysis and synthesis – a profession capable of development, renewal and rigorous intellectual activity in its own right.

My choice of word was deemed somewhat pedantic then, perhaps even unnecessary. After all, were there not words already in use in teacher-training which did the job perfectly well? Words such as 'theory', 'practice', 'methodology'? Surely, these were good enough labels to describe what it was we knew about and taught when we said we worked in teacher-training?

But, in fact, they were not good enough descriptions; unless, that is, the prevailing conditions and attitudes reflected one's own position. My appropriation of the word 'pedagogy' was not intended as just a straight swap for 'tuition', 'method' or 'practice'. Rather, it was to try to encapsulate *unacknowledged* concepts of what teaching was about and what can and should constitute its professional subject matter.

I chose the word 'pedagogy' to name these things because, despite its narrow usage in English, elsewhere in Europe the word has more positive meaning. 'Pedagogy' – meaning the *science* of teaching – lent the activity a certain cachet absolutely in contrast to our own system of thinking about it. In this society, we certainly did not, and still do not, grant the study of teaching the standing of a science, nor the practice of it, the standing of an art form. Indeed, historically, we have defined the study and practice of teaching narrowly and, even if unconsciously, we have arranged things so that the profession and its practitioners have every possible kind of low status conferred upon them. When teaching is so complex a set of practices, when it is so important to the development of individuals and of society, when it is culturally and economically of such importance, how is it that it can be so negatively positioned?

The fundamental answer to this question is to be found in a class analysis of the relationship of teaching to education. As a teacher colleague put it, 'Teaching is for the masses, educating for the classes – upper, of course.'

I want now to draw out some of the strands of the legacy bequeathed us by the hierarchical class reality that lies behind the low status perception so often accorded to the teaching profession and to show how, having entered the collective unconscious, such perceptions in turn contribute to the construction of a system which inhibits and limits both teaching and learning.

One strand of this legacy of what constitutes teaching is nicely reflected in *Roget's Thesaurus* (1853; Penguin abridged edition, 1953), which, being what it is – a classification of words 'according to their signification...', 'arranged so as to facilitate the expression of ideas and to assist literary composition' – mirrors and preserves, through its inclusions and omissions, its groupings and collocations, the received attitudes and cultural meanings of 'teaching'.

Although there is an extensive entry in the *Thesaurus* under 'teaching', our profession is narrowly defined. The lists we are offered are heavy on didacticism and light-to-invisible on teaching/learning as science, art, process. For example, we have 'instruction', 'edification', 'education'; 'pedagogy' – in the narrow English sense of having equivalence with – 'tuition', 'tutelage', 'direction', 'guidance'; 'exercising', 'drilling', 'practising', 'persuading'; 'propaganda', 'indoctrination', 'inculcation'; 'lessons', 'lectures', 'sermons', 'homilies', 'parables', 'discourse'; 'discipline'; 'educate', 'form', 'habituate'. But what is minimal, if indeed it exists at all in the entries, is any reflection of teaching as an understanding of and ability to support pupils through stages of development and achievement. Where are the concept-framing words which indicate that teaching is an integrated set of practices based on understandings of pupils' actual lived experience and modes of learning? Where are the words to indicate teaching as an extensive understanding of educational theory interrelated, in practice, with a wide range of classroom management skills? References in the *Thesaurus* like 'prepare', 'familiarise with', 'nurture', 'initiate', 'direct attention to' and 'guide' would seem the entries approximating most closely to this complex of meanings, to this construction of a facilitative and developmental meaning for teaching, except that they collocate so unfortunately closely with 'break in' and 'tame'.

As for the persons themselves, a teacher is a 'trainer', 'instructor', 'initiator', 'master', 'tutor', 'don', 'director', 'coach', 'crammer', 'governess', 'disciplinarian', 'professor', 'lecturer', 'preacher', 'missionary'. We find that s/he is also a 'guide', 'mentor', 'pioneer', 'example', but again, there is no word or set of words which describes a teacher as one who, as an informed and intellectually rigorous partner to her pupils or students in a context of mutual responsibility, provides for active learning processes which both promote development, skills, knowledge and achievement and also support learners' confidence and independence. Interestingly, 'pedagogue' appears in a subset with 'schoolmaster', 'dominie' and 'usher', while 'schoolmistress' appears in a subset with 'monitor', 'proctor' and 'pupil-teacher'!

With such a long history of the popular association of 'teaching' with notions more akin to training and habituation than with active meaning-making or intention on the part of the learners, it is small wonder that today it is such a battle to redefine 'teaching' as something which legitimately includes facilitative practice. Moreover, it is easy to see how, if teaching is constructed in the collective consciousness as training and habituation, it is only 'natural' that becoming a teacher will involve teacher-trainees in going through, not professional education but something designated, still, as teacher-training, an activity narrowly conceived *and*, in this culture, disparagingly perceived in comparison with academic study. In relation to the low status of the teaching profession, we should not forget that 'training' is the word reserved for the 'education' people are offered if they have not chosen – and for 'have not chosen' read 'are not perceived as up to' – academic work.

This 'normal' construction of teaching as training – and, inescapably, of learning as being trained – has had ideological and methodological consequences. The 'normal', traditional paradigm, which to this day leaves its mark, was overwhelmingly didactic, with pupils positioned minus a truly active role in their learning, and teachers in a reciprocal transmission mode. Teachers' own training followed the same pattern. Thus, not only does the training paradigm fail pupils, but 'trained' teachers contribute to this failure.

To mitigate this, we needed to detach ourselves from notions that preparation for teaching, in-service and further professional development in teaching means *merely* a matter of becoming acquainted with a body of already extant knowledge (theory) and an agreed set of skills and strategies (practice) to which all sensible people subscribe. And we needed to deny that all a person has to do to be a teacher is to learn how to do the set pieces; and that these can be learned like movements in a traditional dance under supervised practice – capable of some manipulation and re-alignment by the trainee, but staying, nevertheless, within a set frame – choreographed by an expert trainer.

This is as true for those undertaking further professional development as it is for initial teacher trainees. Counteraction was necessary because knowledge of teaching (whether for or about it) is neither finite nor capable of being so directly transmitted; neither is the content of the theories chosen for transmission universally recognised as apt for the building of a broad theory of education. Furthermore, the application of skills and strategies just cannot be independent of learning contexts. There may be agreement about general educational principles – if derived from theories of learning development – but there is no good or best practice derivable from the principles without its being grounded in specific contexts.

As for the *concept* of practice: that also needed, and still needs, to be reinterpreted in the light of the differences in outcome between a training mode of learning and an educational mode. Teaching is 'practice' in the sense that what we learn to do is a set of 'practices'. It is also true that teaching is 'practice', in the sense that we learn to do it by 'practising'. But both the 'practices' and the 'practising' are only part of the whole. They do not adequately describe what real teaching is any more than the wordstrings in the *Thesaurus*. For teachers to be able to help pupils achieve and be self-respecting, confident and independent learners, they themselves must surely have courses that provide them with the broadest educational knowledge, skills and understanding of learning development. They must have courses that give them the experience that will enable them to educate, not merely train, their pupils. These things have been impossible to achieve within the practices associated with 'normal' teacher-training.

'Normal' teacher-training was offered in the mode Freire (1972) called 'banking'. Characteristically, it was a componential approach, which maintains strong boundaries between the subjects on the timetable. Typically, such courses had three main strands, Education, Curriculum and Methodology, and Teaching Practice. The first comprised further separate areas, History of Education, Sociology of Education, Psychology of Education and Philosophy of Education, each taught separately by experts in each field. The second, usually taught by someone different again from any of the others so far mentioned, was about the content of the curriculum and about methods of teaching it. Teaching Practice might also have been supervised by an 'unknown' tutor. Certainly, except in a minority of training institutions, it was not supervised by a student's main subject or 'methods' tutor. In this traditional pattern of preparation for teaching, the relationship between the components was not studied. Students were expected to relate in their own minds the range of extant theory to a selected body of knowledge about practice. As a result, theory and practice came to be seen as being in opposition rather than in a complementary and developing relationship. Moreover, theory was not seen to be as relevant as 'practice', a view which has left us with an interminable, damaging and misplaced debate about whether theory is at all relevant to the preparation of teachers.

Although questions about which and what kind of theory and which and what kind of practice certainly arise, the real issue does not lie in this opposition between theory and practice. Rather, it lies in the debilitating consequences for a profession, which should rightfully be based on rigorous thinking, analysis and the development of practice, of raising this false polarity. In recent years, programmes of study of this kind have been designed for teachers' professional education so that links are made between theories, practices, actual teaching contexts and the art of teaching; and it is on these that teacher education should be based.

'Splitting' is not the only limiting factor in 'normal' teacher-training. Other factors, too, reflect back to potential and practising teachers a limited perception of what they can be and do as teachers. For example, critical analysis is experienced by student teachers as a tool of external assessment which emphasises dominance and unequal power relationships, rather than as a tool of ongoing, self-motivated enquiry. Yet teachers need to use critical analysis in this second, educational and developmental way if they are to become the practitioners and theory-makers who are needed to create real achievement for all pupils in the educational settings in which they will do their work.

Yet, what they need could still not be what they get. The 'normal' framework does not legitimate students in this way. It merely positions them as jobbing apprentices: a construction of learning which is no more appropriate to craft apprentices than it is to student teachers.

If teaching has suffered in status from being denied many of its essential features in both popular descriptions *and* professional constructions of it, the final irony is that teaching's low status can also be ascribed to what it must intrinsically be if it is to be successful.

Teaching is an eclectic undertaking, and complexly so, its character frequently arising from putting together often very disparate, even unlikely, concerns related to theory, knowledge, understanding and experience. Yet, while eclecticism *can be* construed as wise and informed choice among relevant concerns or the reconciliation of principles and opinions belonging to different schools of thought and bodies of knowledge, it is just as often construed as a 'butterfly' activity, a picking up of gleanings from here and there. In the academic world it is this second construction which is placed on the activity and which contributes to the positioning of teaching as a low-level intellectual undertaking, inferior in status to 'pure' and 'applied' fields of knowledge and research.

Was Shaw creating or reflecting this view when he reputedly said of teachers, 'Those who can, do; those who can't, teach'? What ignorant nonsense! Only the gate-keeping born of our elitist class system would need to evaluate teachers as failed writers, artists, historians, scientists, mathematicians, athletes, musicians, whatever; or want to rank forms of thinking. Such dominant assumptions obscure the truth that teaching contains within it all the same necessities for on-going, successful outcomes of theory-making and the development of practice as any of the more narrowly and more statically defined fields. Such assumptions also obscure recognition of one of the most rigorous of testing grounds imaginable for any profession: the everyday imperative of the classroom.

Absolutely unacknowledged in these assumptions is the fact that teachers are, in consequence, uniquely positioned to make a rigorous contribution from within the context of their own teaching to important areas of knowledge about teaching and learning. From this point of view, and to paraphrase the title of one of James Baldwin's essays (1985): *If teaching isn't doing, then tell me, what is?*

At present, we work in an inadequate and self-fulfilling system, which builds on the preconditions of under-achievement for pupils, student teachers, teachers and teacher-training establishments. There are well-founded fears that the new National Curriculum, with its hierarchical levels of attainment and its rigid, age-related arrangements for assessment – alongside the reorganisation of funding for initial and in-service courses for teachers – constitutes a reactionary retrenchment which will do all too little to support real achievement either for pupils or teachers. It is not difficult to foresee who will be blamed when failure within the system is perceived yet again.

It is always difficult to work against dominant assumptions, especially when these are held by many within the profession as well as more widely in society. However, if pedagogy, as an area of reflective study, practice, analysis and action research seems still to be a missing concept within the dominant construction of education, the pedagogy principle itself is not missing. It exists, developed over some considerable time by a minority of teachers and educationalists, who have a mind for the intellectual, moral and political commitment to greater equality of opportunity and to greater equality of outcomes in education. The pedagogic medium for the growth and nurture of this praxis within teacher-education has been a continuing *developmental* interaction, with teachers as theory-makers in their own right in reflexive partnership with teacher educators. The product of this dialectic relationship between teachers and teacher educators, and between theory and practice, is an increasingly recognisable area of practical and theoretical knowledge, at once integrative and autonomous.

There is no doubt that the key to improving the state of education at every level – teacher education and teachers' professional status included – is situated within the practices and orientations for which I have reappropriated the word 'pedagogy'.

At a time when the government – with the ostensible purpose of raising standards – enacts decisions which misguidedly emphasise the training paradigm, it would be reprehensible on the part of teacher educators to continue or return to an uncritical maintenance of the same paradigm. What is needed are the reflections and actions that legitimise pedagogy as an area of study and practice.

In teacher education, as in other areas of teaching, what we *do* is what we teach.

References

Baldwin, James (1985) *The Price of the Ticket: collected non-fiction 1948-1985*, Michael Joseph

Freire, Paulo (1972) *Pedagogy of the Oppressed*, Penguin

Chapter 9

Development pedagogy: alternative strategies for multilingual classrooms

It would be difficult to overestimate the importance of Vygotskian theory to our concerns. Vygotsky offers a theory of intellectual development which accounts for children's progress in terms of their interaction – joint activity and conversation – with other people, the adults and peers with whom they have contact. The structures of these encounters, the medium in which they take place, the culture(s) in which they are embedded, the meanings with which they are imbued are taken inwards, internalised, through the process of interaction. Being complex sets of interrelated features, taking their meanings from their relatedness as much, if not more, than from the individual components, interaction provides multilayered, connected material from which participants with a wide range of experience can extract different kinds of knowledge and skills according to their needs. At the same time, they come into contact with, and therefore preparation for, the next and successive phases of their development. Finally, being developmental, such learning is incremental in the sense that learners, young and old, are also always in states of approximation toward the thing or things which are being learned and/or developed (Levine, 1990 pp.289-290).

Overview

The basic proposition is straightforward. Multilingual classrooms have obvious potential for the development of English as an additional language. However, the history of trying to turn that potential into reality has been anything but straightforward. It is a history riddled with race, class, cultural and linguistic prejudice, a history of both official and unofficial obstruction to educational development – indeed a classic case of blindness on the part of education to its own provision of *unequal* opportunities. Consequently, theory, practice and principles for the countering of this situation have been initiated and developed from positions of opposition to the educational status quo. Progress has been made, but by no means enough of it for the present situation to be a happy one. Equal opportunities education strives, therefore, to be about the entitlement rhetoric promises, but does not deliver, ie about supposed equal rights of access to a meaningful curriculum, to cultural and linguistic respect, to high expectation of achievement and to greater equality of outcomes for all the social groups against which historic prejudices have worked.

Amongst these groups are children of ethnic minority origin who are learning English as an additional language – the majority of whom are also working class. For the majority of them, their education takes place in multilingual classrooms, but unfortunately, very often in an ethos where the rich potential of such classrooms for developing English as an additional language is seriously underdeveloped. However, it is in some of these classrooms that the model for the development of such potential has been shaped.

In the course of this chapter, an emergent good practice is described for a morally responsible, equal opportunities education. Essentially Vygotskian in character, being both interactive and developmental, it is referred to as 'developmental pedagogy'. At the heart of the development of this pedagogy in Britain are a significant minority of teachers in multilingual classrooms.

This developmental pedagogy draws on Vygotskian ideas about:

- the relationship between cognitive and linguistic development in the 'native language'

- the role of social and reflective processes in learning development

- the relationship between teaching ('instruction') and learning ('development of concepts').

At the heart of this pedagogy is a dialectic comprising:

- internalisation as a result of interaction

- conscious awareness resulting from teaching intervention

- the learning processes of reflection and analysis.

When multilingual classrooms are actual sites of interactive, analytic, reflective learning; when the learning environment is supportive *and* rigorous; when, through a pedagogically flexible response to cultural and linguistic diversity, wider access to learning is achieved; when bilingual learners are encouraged to use all their linguistic resources in school, then we have an educational and linguistic environment which allows additional language learning to be a 'normal' part of learning. It is this 'normalised' language learning, within the freedom and rigour of a broad *curricula provision*, that is essential to the achievement of true educational entitlement for bilingual pupils.

What lies behind this assertion are some obvious, but educationally and linguistically underexploited, contextual truths. Bilingual learners in multilingual classes in Britain are learning to use English as an additional language for central purposes in their lives. They do so in a context where the target language is both the dominant language in society *and* the medium of instruction in school. In other words, they have real purpose for acquiring the target language and they have living access to it. Furthermore, consonant with their age and experience, they already have a more developed use of at least one other language. It makes both human and pedagogic sense to use the natural features of pupils' lives to build an educational context out of what they have natural access to and out of what they already know and can do, rather than to continue with methodologies that deny them these natural learning 'aids'.

In the context of bilingual pupils' learning of English, it is this 'naturalised' orientation for learning *and* for additional language learning and development which I see as a superior basis for formulating a theory and practice for successful additional language learning, and indeed, not only for bilingual pupils.

Conflicts and tensions

When children came to the UK speaking a range of languages other than English, they were not perceived as already experienced users of language, competent communicators about to start a new phase of their lives – a phase in which they would begin to add an *additional* language, English, to their repertoires. Instead, they were regarded as being in linguistic and cultural deficit. Their previous languages and learning experiences were ignored; their cultural backgrounds were seen as irrelevant to English schooling; they found themselves disparagingly dubbed 'non-English speakers', sometimes even, 'children with no language', 'beginner learners' (and not just of English) – and they were regarded as unequipped for participation in 'normal' classrooms. The education system perceived as paramount the need to learn English, and to learn it discretely, separated from their other curricular learning. Once the newcomers had learned English, *then* they would be allowed to learn the 'other' subjects.

So, 'Special English' classes were established and bilingual pupils were then described, not as pupils of English, Maths, Geography or whatever, but as 'learners of English as a second language', 'E2L kids', terms which, in effect, reflected the linguistic and cultural prejudice of the dominant social group. 'Special English' classes were taught primarily on the basis of withdrawal from the mainstream curriculum. Thus, within the already existing hierarchical organisation of British schooling, these children were yet further marginalised. As a result, even the positive functions these 'special' classes performed were soon outweighed by the

structural effect such classes inevitably had in compounding the conditions of underachievement already established by the educational
system for the majority of working-class pupils.

Recently the term 'bilingual pupils' has begun to be used, and more
recently still, the phrase 'pupils acquiring English as an additional
language'. The term 'multilingual classrooms' came into use prior to
these, as some kind of acknowledgement that it was normal to have many
languages represented in one classroom. However, the description does
not refer to multilanguage *use* in these classrooms but only to the range of
languages spoken by the pupils, not in school, but at home.

These newer terms genuinely offer a more accurate construction of
bilingual pupils:

- as developing learners

- to be understood and valued as already competent and knowledgeable

- with what they know, including their linguistic prowess productively
  linked with their present and future learning

- with their English language learning enterprise being about developing a linguistic repertoire that adds to rather than replaces already
  known languages.

Nevertheless, even the newer terms are suspect, and the reasons for
suspicion are currently not hard to find. With so great a weight being
placed on the use of Standard English in the National Curriculum, with
bilingualism and the right to use one's first language recognised as a
prerogative of Welsh schools only (DES, 1989), with so much political
emphasis on 'our' national heritage, it would seem that the linguistic
communities of Britain's ethnic minorities are likely to continue to experience the downgrading of their languages in relation to English.
Consequently, we can also anticipate that schools are likely to continue to
underachieve in meeting the intellectual and skill development needs of
their bilingual pupils.

Even where there is belated recognition of bilingual pupils as not deficient but as pupils developing both their learning and their bilingual proficiency, the issue of ethnic minority pupils' rights to bilingual education remains beyond the pale. Bilingual education would be feasible to develop where one community language dominates, as is the case for Welsh speakers, but there is virtually no support for it via political will or vision within the educational system. The fact of the matter is that even in multicultural and multilingual classrooms our educational culture is such that there are relatively few classrooms where teachers are fully committed to developing the sort of interactive pedagogies that are, I argue, the only honest means of achieving equal opportunities education for pupils suffering the social class, gender, ethnocentric and linguistic discrimination of the British educational system.

In consequence, there is manifest tension between the possible and the actual in multilingual classrooms, which is not eased by the continuing presence of traditional forms of restrictive thinking about language and education. For example:

- continued questioning of bilingualism set against the goal of learning English as an additional language, *as though one must necessarily exclude or diminish the value of the other*;

- bilingualism set against the feasibility of successful curriculum learning, *as though it was inconceivable that a pedagogy could be developed which took advantage of linking learning and language development*;

- linguistic and cultural diversity set against 'British culture and language', *as though there was no relationship between such sectionalism and the systematic exclusion from curricular success of British working-class culture, interests and forms of thinking*.

Assuredly, the downgrading of pupils' bilingualism and the constraints of withdrawal classes on pupils' access to the mainstream curriculum contribute to pupils' underachievement in school, and as such, are components of institutionalised racial and class discrimination. This discrimination within the education system constitutes the most successful and longstanding con trick perpetrated by 'education'.

Race and class prejudice and the educational offer in multilingual classrooms

Working-class children and bilingual learners in English schools have both had a poor deal. This is because the educational base has always been a diverse, class-ridden system promoting the type of education most accessible to the dominant power group, and in which, broadly speaking, achievement has depended either on pupils originating in the middle classes, or – in keeping with the meritocratic ideal – on being able and willing to espouse its precepts.

Despite the fact that class is a consistently acknowledged factor in success and failure in the school system, the obvious conclusion is equally consistently evaded: that an education system founded and maintained along class dimensions is intrinsically structured against groups with cultural and intellectual traditions different from the hegemonic 'norm'. Failure within the system is seen as residing in those against whom the system is most prejudiced, those at the bottom of the class and culture hierarchy. It is their 'backgrounds' which assign them to educational failure, not the educational system itself.

The different types of schools (public vs state; grammar vs technical *vs* secondary modern) have functioned historically to separate the different groups in society on grounds of birth, money and parental and/or intended profession. Furthermore, within the hierarchy of the system, streaming had been used across all types of schooling to *further* differentiate, delineate and maintain boundaries between socio-economic groups on the basis of children's 'ability' as measured by the 'norms' of the system. The attempt to rank groups to such a degree of homogeneity invariably led to every school having its 'Remove' classes, its remedial sub-system, for those who could not, or would not, cope.

It was into this educational system that bilingual pupils came. As with working-class children, they were required to acquire, along with their English, the linguistic modes and forms of thought which formed the world view characteristic of the dominant class minority within the population. Within the structures and practices of such a 'class-centric' curriculum, a whole range of stratifications, qualitative differences, within the educational offer existed. 'Education' became a successive watering down of the dominant class's curriculum, each successive dilution being the means by which pupils were deemed to be receiving the education 'suited to their age, ability and aptitude'. For example, those who had not passed the old 11+ examination, 80 per cent of the population, had successive stages of 'access' to the least rigorous version of a curriculum which, by virtue of its starting point, neither met their intellectual needs nor acknowledged (let alone ascribed status to) their interests, forms of thinking, or their cultural presence.

Language education played its part in this constructed lack of opportunity for the majority population. Faithful to the elitist tradition outlined above, language education for most pupils was, in effect, about learning 'correct' English. In fact, modern foreign language learning was, for most pupils, conspicuous by its absence in their curriculum. Only the 'clever' kids had access to additional language learning – the cleverest of all to the elitist prize of Latin and Greek. This elitism must surely be a basic factor in any account of the failure of the British people generally to acquire additional languages.

Provision for the bilingual youngsters who were yet to develop English as an additional language was mapped onto this deeply divisive structure, with inherent race prejudice mapped onto the legacy of class prejudice. Almost automatically those who could not speak English were ranked at the bottom of the pile, their cultural backgrounds and linguistic abilities not only ignored but regarded as a hindrance to both their progress in English and their achievement in school.

Given the then existing standard language teaching practices (structural-grammatical; behaviouristic methodology) and the so limited experience of the British people of *natural* second or foreign language learning, inevitably, provision for the newcomers was made on the basis of the simplistic assumptions that pupils would need to know English *before* they could or *should* participate in 'normal' classes. The narrowly defined, 'correct', *linguistic* aspects of the curriculum were seen as both separate from and prior to *educational* aspects. Thus did 'Special English' lessons fit into an already existing educational culture of streaming and withdrawal. Notwithstanding the commitment, caring and concern of so many of these 'Special English' teachers towards their pupils, the overall system was clearly a disadvantaging one.

Indeed, no better design could have been conceived for denying bilingual learners in English schools the conditions of success. They were deprived by the established structures and practices of schooling of curricular access to precisely those areas of experience and linguistic interaction for which they were so earnestly, but nevertheless inadequately, being prepared in their 'Special English' classes. On top of this, they were separated from use of their mother-tongues by virtue of ethnocentrism, by power-play (how would teachers and other pupils know what their pupils were doing or saying if they did not speak English in class?) and by shiboleths about language learning (mother tongues seen as interfering with learning a new language). Basically, *all* school children were being told that the English language in its standard forms, and English people – particularly those with 'received' accents – were superior to other languages and people.

Antipathetic to the interests of all working-class children and to bilingual learners in particular, these were policies for *mis*education. Practice and policy acted to structure underachievement; to construct and/or confirm racist attitudes among the school population; and to maintain narrow attitudes to language education in the whole of society. Linguistic imperialism was encouraged; bi- and multi-lingualism discouraged. And in using primarily the methods of teaching English as a *foreign*, rather than as a second language, the isolation of 'Special English' from subject teaching and curriculum learning was preserved and strengthened.

This combination of the establishment of a category of 'Special English' teachers teaching separately from the mainstream curriculum and using the traditions of *foreign* language teaching conspired to delay the development of strategies, techniques and pedagogies designed to meet the mainstream and real language needs of bilingual learners. Separation also seriously delayed the establishment of fruitful links between those 'Special English' teachers who were trying to develop more appropriate language teaching strategies and mainstream teachers who *were* developing mixed ability language across the curriculum pedagogies.

This delay has been especially galling when one considers what the two movements hold in common for creating improved teaching methods for *all* children and, therefore, equality of outcome for the working-class majority, black, white, girls and bilingual learners. Both movements have constructed pedagogies stemming from recognition of the generative power of the relationships between language, experience and learning. Both movements seek positively to incorporate, rather than counter-productively deny, the truly intellectually rigorous *social* contexts of learning, the *necessity* of such a context for developing knowledge in depth, skills and understanding. Both movements recognise how disabling it is for learners if the learning environment separates them from what they already know and can already do.

Nevertheless, despite the very considerable structural divisions between these two sets of teachers, partnerships have been instituted amongst teachers who are morally, politically and intellectually committed to rigorous equal opportunities education. Sadly, they still have to work against ignorance of the cognitive links between first and second language development and between these and learning development.

Despite the enormous growth of knowledge about language (about its interactive as well as grammatical structures, about the essential social base of language acquisition and development, about the relationships between thought, language and learning, about its use as a means of individual empowerment, and its function as a tool of control and oppression), it is not this newer, more relevant pedagogic and linguistic knowledge which has *fundamentally* influenced any of the reformist policy proposals contained in the National Curriculum, although ghostly traces of it can be seen there.

No better examples of the maintenance of a narrow view of language, and of the 'ghostliness' of new knowledge within the reforms can be found than in the language model offered by the Committee of Enquiry into the Teaching of the English Language (DES, 1988) and in the consequent proposals for English in the National Curriculum for ages 5 to 16 (DES, 1989).

Despite the National Curriculum proposing committee's pragmatically finer intentions, (basically) the National Curriculum for English sings an all too familiar refrain. Dangers lurk within the National Curriculum for all pupils membershipped to multilingual classes. For example, despite the careful statement in the *National Curriculum Proposals* (DES, 1989: 4.14) that all languages and dialects are rule governed, that their rules differ, and that it is not the case that Standard English possesses rules and the others do not, the effect of the repeated exhortation to teach Standard English is to affirm the historic position of the English establishment that English is superior to other languages and Standard English to other varieties of English. *The National Curriculum Proposals* are also inherently undermining of their own purported support both for a broad approach to languages and for teaching which acknowledges and supports 'a firmly based but flexible and developing linguistic and cultural identity' (DES, 1989: 2.12). In section 10.10 the implication is that pupils' mother tongues will function only as a bridge to their competence in English, and, although in section 3.11 we are invited to view bilingual pupils as an 'enormous resource', this turns out to be significant only insofar as their knowledge of languages can inform *other pupils'* knowledge about *English* (DES, 1989:10.12).

Clearly, the past is ever with us, and never more so than in the proposals for assessment in the National Curriculum. No obeisance to the notion of cultural diversity can overcome the downright inequity inherent in such forms of assessment. The fact that the Speaking and Listening Attainment Targets (where bilingual pupils in the process of acquiring English were more likely to have been able to be assessed as achieving more of the aspects of achievement than for the Reading and Writing Attainment Targets) were omitted from the first National Attainment Tests is one more example of structured inequity.

On the other hand, the fact that Speaking and Listening is a focus for attainment along with Reading and Writing in the National Curriculum should mean an increase in teachers' understanding of the importance of *talking to learn*. This has the potential for contributing to the communicative and interactive base essential to naturalising learning for everyone. However, as the London Association for the Teaching of English notes in its *Responses to English from Ages 11-16* (1989), 'the nuances are wrong'. Whatever good, interactive pedagogy teachers manage to preserve, or even the requirements of the National Curriculum happen to promote, assessment of pupils within a rigid level of attainment – based on assumptions of learning and language development being an organised series of linear progressions – disallows wider acknowledgement of pupils' actual potential. Bilingual pupils inexperienced in using English will be confirmed as low achievers in language and learning, and other working-class pupils, their culture and language also highly constrained, will also be so confirmed, with consequent further low expectations virtually assured. Slotting pupils into 'levels' is but a few steps away from the wholesale reconstitution of streaming and an over-use of 'Special English' withdrawal teaching and of 'Remedial' classes – all of which are intellectually and educationally crude and politically simplistic ways of making provision for pupils' 'differentiated learning needs'.

If fears about the effects of the statutory requirements of the National Curriculum on bilingual pupils in the process of learning English needed confirming, confirmation is found in the timing and the content of the National Curriculum Council's leaflet *Circular Number 11: The Needs of Bilingual Pupils* (NCC, 1991). This was published just prior to the onset of the first application of assessment at Key Stage 1, as the anticipated dangers were becoming ever more clearly defined. It urges schools to consider both 'how to ensure full access to the National Curriculum and Assessments for all pupils' and also to value languages other than English spoken by pupils and used in the classroom' (NCC, 1991). It emphasises:

- that 'language teaching is the professional responsibility of all teachers'

- that 'the National Curriculum is for all pupils except the few for whom modification and disapplication is appropriate'

- that 'like all pupils, bilingual pupils should have access to stimulating curriculum which, at the same time, helps their language development'

- that 'bilingual children are able to understand and develop concepts even when their ability to express them in English is limited [in support of which they quote evidence given to the National Curriculum English Working Group] 'where bilingual children need extra help, this should be given as part of normal lessons' adding that 'withdrawal of bilingual pupils for separate teaching . . . can lead to a narrow, unbalanced curriculum and [to] isolation from pupils with greater experience of English' (NCC, 1991).

All of this, the circular stresses, means beginning with present good practice (developed, I remind you, in multilingual classrooms). Some helpful suggestions follow. For example:

work can be carried out in different language and peer groups to encourage the use of preferred languages, or in multilingual groups to help pupils benefit from the experience of other languages. This would enable the teacher to observe and identify where language support is needed (NCC, 1991).

I do not draw attention to this leaflet in order to question whether or not these pragmatic hints about good practice are necessary; of course, they are. The question is, rather, whether such hints on their own are sufficient

117

to amount to a *good enough* practice; and, of course, they are not. What is needed is an indepth practice, one that goes well beyond the hints of the NCC leaflet.

Such in-depth good practice exists. What is needed now is for it to be more widely recognised, more widely practised and further developed.

Developmental pedagogy: alternative strategy for multilingual classrooms

Multilingual classrooms, although not alone in acting as prompts to pedagogic development, have obviously been *the* significant site for the development of an equal opportunities education. Such classrooms were perceived by many teachers as threatening, but for others the existence of such dynamic classrooms provided the creative disruption to the educational status quo which allowed them to take the practical and theoretical steps necessary for establishing egalitarian frames of reference in the support of learning.

These theoretical and practical frames of reference hold that the goal of educational development and achievement is most effectively attained through social and intellectual processes conceived as partnerships between the participants. Such a partnership orientation is one in which successive stages of development are seen as the outcomes of the processes of experimental methodology which, in turn, are open to reflection, analysis and further development by its practitioners. A strong element of teachers' action research is thus an integral component of successful teaching and learning within this practice.

Educational partnerships are conceived as dynamic and dialectical learning relationships. Their aim is the promotion and development of skills, supportiveness, intellectual rigour, meaning and mutuality. Pupils' language and learning repertoires grow both by means of their participation in meaningful interaction with other people, with resources and texts, and by direct instruction.

Organisationally, classroom partnerships tend to fall into three, interrelated categories.

1. *Pupils working and learning in pairs and/or small groups* (often called 'collaborative learning').

2. *Teachers* working with pupils as a whole class group, or with individuals, pairs or small groups in an instructional and/or facilitating role.

3. *Teachers planning and working together to support pupils' learning*, sometimes planning materials and strategies together prior to lessons, sometimes teaching together (often called 'support teaching', 'co-operative teaching' and most recently 'partnership teaching').

Such partnerships, when taken in conjunction with curriculum content, materials and assignments which attend to the sociocultural aspects of the development, acquisition and application of knowledge, have the potential for advantaging learning in several crucial ways.

- Partnerships between pupils and between pupils and teachers, being naturally various, but also appropriately structured, provide many subtly differing language-saturated and, therefore, rich language learning environments.

- Such partnerships enable responsibility for the curriculum enterprise to be shared, as appropriate, between the various participants – pupils and teachers alike.

- Participants' own histories, skills, knowledge, forms of thinking and language enter the classroom, and through that validation, learners' confidence may be founded, maintained and developed.

- Learning proceeds dialectically. That is, participants' already internalised skills and knowledge, together with those more conscious analytic processes motivated by new experience and challenge, both form the shared learning ground and contribute to each individual's change and growth.

- Being active settings for gaining knowledge and developing skills, partnerships provide an educational environment akin to the socially interactive context in which participants have experienced their 'natural' learning. Concepts, skills, knowledge, linguistic repertoire, analytic competence, the confidence to be oppositional as well as to build consensus, may all develop in relation to the quality of the social process.

• Partnerships provide pupils and teachers with a greater variety of roles. In consequence, they are better positioned to understand 'where each is coming from', and to know the steps which will enable each to achieve learning goals. The 'us and them' battle lines of the traditional classroom are diminished and can be replaced by an inclusive social-learning grouping of 'we', which at the same time supports differences of need and of identity.

• Within the concept of partnership, pupils' school learning and the art of teaching may be seen as productively and creatively linked, both subject to the same 'rules' of development in relation to progress and achievement.

• Both learning and language internalisation are facilitated by participation.

Developmental pedagogy: starting points and developmental steps

Clearly, such a developmental pedagogy has a Vygotskian ring to it, and yet I have written nothing yet in reference to his thinking about the social origin and nature of learning. Nor yet have I sought to comment on his positioning in *Thought and Language* (1962/1988) of foreign language learning. This is because I have needed to set the context of multilingual classrooms as rich sites for learning and for learning English as an additional language. It is also because without this contextualising it would be difficult for those who do not have direct experience of partner-shipped developmental pedagogy at work to visualise the complex inter-relations of factors in such classrooms. For example:

- the role of *language* in learning

- the role of *learning* in language development

- the role of *interaction* in the internalisation of knowledge and skills – including linguistic skills

- the relationship of *learning* to first and second language development

- the relationship of first and second language development to *each other.*

But, principally, I have not yet related developmental pedagogy to Vygotsky's theory of learning and development because it is essential to acknowledge the pre-eminent role of teachers in establishing the practice of this interactive pedagogy and also to recognise that pedagogic developments do not arise only out of consciously held theory, in fact, sometimes not at all. Teachers develop theories as much as theories develop them. Teachers initiate practice on the basis of their own analyses of experience – often against the theories of learning and development with which they came in contact in their training. When they then find an account of learning development which matches closely and *explains* the precepts by which they were already working and which they were working towards, they enter into a dialectic relationship with these theories of learning.

Developmental pedagogy, itself in dialectical relationship to Vygotsky's theories of socially based interactive learning, has come about through a conjunction of significant movements and activities, each of which had separate starting points:

1. teaching and learning activities directed at combating race, class and gender prejudice in educational organisation and curricula;

2. that branch of activity within the field of teaching English as a second language in multicultural schools which took its inspiration from generative theories about language (eg Chomsky, 1965), ideas about linguistic and communicative competence (eg Chomsky, 1965; Hymes, 1971), and the relationship of function and form in language

(eg Halliday, 1969, 1970, 1971), in order to develop practices for the *communicative* teaching of English as a second language;

3. the development of mixed ability teaching.

What teachers of English in the comprehensive school/mixed ability teaching movement found particularly productive in Vygotsky's ideas about linguistic and cognitive development and their relationship to each other were:

* *the setting of intellectual development in* social *activity* ('In our conception, the true direction of the development of thinking is not from the individual to the socialised, but from the social to the individual' (Vygotsky, 1962/1988: 20). 'The child's intellectual growth is contingent on his mastering the social means of thought, that is, language' (1962/1988: 51). 'What the child can do in co-operation today he can do alone tomorrow' (1962/1988: 41).

* *the centrality given to* meaning and communication *as motivators for learning, thus positioning talk as the most widely accessible starting point for learning* ('The primary function of speech is communication, social intercourse; and 'the development of understanding and communication in childhood . . . has led to the conclusion that *real communication* requires meaning' (1962/1988: 6, my italics)).

* *the relationship made between* teaching and learning development ('...the only good kind of instruction is that which marches ahead of development and leads it; it must not be aimed so much at the ripe as at the ripening functions'. 'Our investigation demonstrated the social and cultural nature of development of the higher functions during (schooling), ie its dependence on co-operation with adults and on instruction' (1962/1988:104, 105). This is crystallised in Vygotsky's concept of the 'zone of proximal development'. ('...the distance between the actual development level as determined by independent problem-solving and the level of potential development as determined

through problem-solving under adult guidance or in collaboration with more capable peers' (Vygotsky, 1978:86)).

- *the highlighting of* conscious reflection *as a generator of development.*

Later, as the practice of developmental pedagogy began to grow, the importance to it of Vygotsky's own methodological approach to the analysis of the relationship between thought and language (analysis of whole units as opposed to analysis of the separate elements of wholes) provided a model for a holistic approach to teaching and learning. ('Unit analysis... demonstrates the existence of a dynamic system of meaning in which the affective and the intellectual unite' (Vygotsky, 1962/1988: 81)).

However, the theory being developed in the early 'Vygotskian' classroom was a theory of development for and in *English as Mother Tongue*. At that point, bilingual learners and additional language learning were not seen as coming within its scope. Of course, bilingual pupils were registered students in these classrooms, but they were metaphorically as well as literally as much out of them as in them, withdrawn from the 'normal' mainstream class to 'Special English.'

At the same time, there were teachers in the 'Special English' service seeking mainstream education for bilingual pupils. They realised that if their charges were ever to learn English well enough to take their rightful places as learners within normal classrooms, they needed not discrete and often 'behaviouristic' language teaching but food for their minds. Later, they also came to realise that the curriculum and bilingualism were, in fact, not divisible.

These teachers began to develop techniques for teaching English which combined curriculum learning and additional language teaching techniques in a linguistically interactive approach to learning influenced not by Vygotsky, but by:

- communicative-functional theories of language learning (thinking based on the development of linguistic and communicative competence and on a *functional* approach to understanding language in use, e.g. Chomsky, Hymes, Halliday);

- ideas about learners' interlanguage in their progress towards facility in a target language (L2, L3, ...) ie that any linguistic state mani-fested can be analysed as representing an ordered set of 'rules' whereby performance is generated (eg Selinker, 1972);

- the concept of Error Analysis (in which learners' errors are viewed as part of the adaptive process towards the target language (Corder, 1967, 1971; Richards, 1974)).

Using this communicative approach to additional language learning, teachers began to note that the stages of development through which pupils passed – including the 'errors' they made – frequently paralleled those of early language development. Supported by the linguistic ideas itemised above, teachers began to follow their professional analytical instincts and to view learners' errors as developmental, rather than failed learning.

It seemed profitable to consider what might be gained from looking at how communicative competence is attained in one's first language and to relate this to promoting competence in a second language. I chose at the time to put it this way (Levine, 1972):

When we learn to use our first language, we do so through exposure to performance of it and in response to the demands and requirements of a variety of situations, roles, relationships and mores in which and according to which we live our lives. In so far as communicative competence equates with having learned language behaviour which is both appropriate and effective for the context of our lives, we all probably learn what we are able to do – no matter how different that is in kind or extent – in much the same way. That is to say, we are, and have been, open to external stimulae and motivation to learn the code and its appropriate use while, at the same time, having the opportunity to exercise an innate drive to learn on the code and on the situations and contexts in which particular parts of it are used. Among the elements available external to ourselves are:

(a)   situations which 'direct' us towards certain kinds of language behaviour,

(b)   recurring opportunities within situations to hear, imitate and practise,

(c)   informants who, by their reactions, 'tell' us if we have transmitted our intentions,

(d)   informants and contexts which provide models for us,

(e)   informants who teach and correct us.

Among the 'magic' elements which we bring to the situation ourselves are:

(f)   the ability to store chunks of the data of performance for appropriate repetition,

(g)   our own drive to learn, play, practise, imitate,

(h)   the ability to discern underlying systems of rules,

(i)   the ability to organise and categorise the data of performance in such a way that we can (to paraphrase Chomsky (1965) both understand discourse which we have never heard before and also generate entirely novel utterances of our own without having been exposed to all and every utterance in all and every context in which the utterance might occur.

If these observations are applied to the communicative teaching of an additional language, it must surely suggest a more active role for learners in the learning-teaching process, and a more interactive one, allowing development from the data of the environment.

The history of mixed ability teaching in comprehensive schools, and the history of English as a second language meant that interactive teaching and learning practices for English mother tongue pupils in mixed ability mainstream classes *and* the communicative practices for learning English as a second language came to be developed in parallel, but separately from each other. The two movements began to become more integrated within the policy of supporting the learning of English as an additional language within the mainstream (see Bourne, 1989; Levine, 1990).

As we work to refine the practices of an interactive, socially based, developmental learning theory, it becomes increasingly obvious that such a practice is Vygotskian in character. Instruction aimed at conscious grasp of concepts, knowledge, skills and understanding is in dynamic relationship with, and not in opposition to, natural social and intellectual development. It offers teachers a naturalistic methodology which can put achievement within the reach of many *more* working-class pupils. In this sense, the Vygotskian orientation within pedagogy is not only social, it is socialist.

Vygotsky and the learning of additional languages

Clearly, I do not consider it useful to think of bilingual pupils in multilingual classrooms as learning or being taught English as if it were a foreign language. It is not simply that the *foreign* languages curriculum has historically been characterised by:

1. subject matter and settings extrinsic to the actual social context of additional language learners;

2. syllabuses based on grammatical 'progressions', arbitrarily chosen;

3. teaching practices based largely on linguistic constructions, rather than primarily on what motivates pupils to learn.

It is, rather and quite fundamentally, that foreign languages are regarded in English culture as 'other' – not being, or needing to be, embedded in the lives of the learners – quite literally 'foreign'.

Of course, people in the UK have learned to use additional languages under this foreign language teaching regime but, as a percentage of our population, these are comparatively very few. Fewer still would claim extensive and flexible use of the language(s) they were taught. In fact, most have been put off learning languages and think of it as a difficult thing to do. How contrary the educational system has been, then, towards the bilingual learners in our schools, for while it is always said that they have a right (more a duty) to become fluent, confident users of English, by and large they have been taught English in the discourse of this historical, 'foreign', (disembedded) practice.

But bilingual pupils are not learning English as a foreign language. They live within the boundaries of the additional language's permeating influence. They have personal access to it. It does not have to be 'given' to them by teachers as their *only* means of contact with it. Pupils have a pressing need to learn it for a wide range of social, educational, pragmatic and heuristic functions. It is the medium of instruction in schools and the dominant language in society. They are going to have to do much more with it than mere translation into it from their first languages. They are going to need to move into the 'deep' language acquisition that the knowing of any language as a genuine 'second' language implies, i.e. they need to go well beyond the stage of translation characteristic of attempts to use a studied, but unfamiliar, foreign language.

Progress has, of course, been made, for example by the development of mainstreaming. But, whilst in theory, mainstreaming is now a widely accepted organisational strategy, in practice the tug of withdrawal for 'Special English' is still strong, and still quite widely used as the major organisational strategy in teaching bilingual learners. The tug is strongest of all where interactive developmental pedagogy in the mainstream is weakest. Problems also arise where false dichotomies are established, as for example, between mainstreaming and withdrawal, where mainstreaming is made to mean that there shall be *no* withdrawal teaching. Yet mainstreaming does not rule out *certain kinds* of withdrawal at certain points. There will still be occasions when teaching groups of bilingual learners together will be appropriate, just as it is appropriate upon occasion to work with other kinds of small groups. However, if the shift towards greater enactment of equal opportunities education is to be more than rhetoric, then what needs to be guarded against are withdrawal practices that overwhelm or marginalise mainstreaming. What is needed is an unequivocal acknowledgement of the learning and using of an additional language in educational social reality, and a commitment to going beyond a brief, early 'pastoral' support for incoming bilingual students to offering an in-depth and continuing developmental pedagogy for mainstream curriculum learning.

We also need to continue to identify the detailed processes of interaction, learning and teaching by which bilingual pupils may most effectively develop their use of English within the curriculum. The simple fact that learners are present in the linguistic context cannot itself ensure success – as the 'osmosis' school of 'thought' might suggest. We do not achieve deep learning of languages just because the range of features of the whole language exist in our environment. Neither the 'osmosis' nor the 'special' add-on language teaching 'theory' of putting the second language learning as a separate subject on the timetable, serves our pupils' true needs and purposes. (Indeed, even contemporary functional communicative strategies for teaching modern foreign languages do not easily transform into successful second language learning strategies – except when language and learning *and* thinking are *dynamically interrelated*.)

We need to maintain and develop the focus of languages development being an *integral* part of education, achieved *through* it rather than prior to or disembedded from it. And for bilingual learners, the development of additional language learning practices needs to be based upon the fact that we have a situation more akin to the *contextualised and naturalised* ways in which first languages are developed.

But what does Vygotsky have to say about this?

In *Thought and Language* (1962/1988) he refers only to learning foreign languages under taught, disembedded conditions. The case he makes for formal learning of foreign languages bears inspection, lest it is employed uncritically to support old-fashioned non-communicative language teaching practice.

In the chapter 'The development of scientific concepts in childhood' in *Thought and Language*, Vygotsky assumes the virtues of learning foreign languages in a disembedded way. Even while he quotes Tolstoy on the uselessness of teachers attempting to transfer concepts directly to their pupils through explanation, he appears to find this method acceptable when employed in foreign language teaching. '[Tolstoy] found that one could not teach children literary language by artificial explanations, compulsive memorising, and repetition *as one does a foreign language*' (Vygotsky 1962/1988: 83, my italics).

In the same chapter, it is possible to interpret another reference to foreign languages as further, serious support for disembedded learning of foreign languages. 'The influence of scientific concepts on the mental development of the child is analogous to the effect of learning a foreign language, *a process which is conscious and deliberate from the start*' (Vygotsky 1962/1988:109, my italics).

He then goes on to describe how in foreign language learning, as is indeed the case, one is aware of phonetic, grammatical and syntactic forms before one develops spontaneous, fluent speech. But Vygotsky then takes for granted that it is through study alone that we attain this fluency.

The child's strong points in a foreign language are his weak points in his native language, and vice versa. In his own language, the child conjugates and declines correctly, but without realising it. He cannot tell the gender, the case, or the tense of a word he is using. In a foreign language he distinguishes between masculine and feminine gender and is conscious of grammatical forms from the beginning. Of phonetics the same is true. Faultlessly articulating his native language, the child is unconscious of the sounds he pronounces, and in learning to spell he has great difficulty in dividing a word into its constituent sounds. In a foreign language he does this easily and his writing does not lag behind his speech. It is the pronunciation, the spontaneous phonetics that he finds harder to master. Easy, spontaneous speech with a quick and sure command of grammatical structures comes to him only as the crowning achievement of *long, arduous study* (Vygotsky 1962/1988: 109, my italics).

This suggests a presupposition on Vygotsky's part of a *necessity* to teach a foreign language via 'academic' methods, and that it is *because* of these means that access is also gained to those cognitive benefits which are such highly prized outcomes of knowing more than one language, benefits that ensue for learners in relation to both knowledge *of* languages and *about* language.

> ... a foreign language facilitates mastering the higher forms of the native language, [and] the child learns to see his native language as one particular system among many, to view its phenomena under more general categories, and this leads to awareness of his linguistic operations (Vygotsky 1962/1988: 110).

These statements would not only seem to make 'success in learning a foreign language ... contingent on a certain degree of maturity in the native language', but would also assume in the learner 'transfer to the new language [of] the system of meanings he already possesses in his own' (Vygotsky 1962/1988: 110).

When taken together, a possible reading of these passages for languages *teaching* is that:

- foreign languages *need* – for the sake of cognitive development – to be taught in a disembedded manner

- that the teaching of a foreign language *should* be more concerned with the new language's external manifestations than with semantic aspects – since meaning systems have already been constructed by learners in the acquisition of their first languages

- and, remaining with this same point, that children might not be able to learn a foreign language well unless they have what is considered to be a degree of maturity in their first language.

As readers will recognise, such strands of thought are familiar ones within the theories and practices of foreign language teaching. How curiously at variance they are with the deeper meanings that imbue the developmental pedagogy I have outlined in an earlier section, the pedagogy which teachers have constructed (consciously and unconsciously) and which owes so much to Vygotsky's central theory about the relationship between speech and thought and the *social* roots of their development.

It is therefore worth taking a second look, this time at the positioning of Vygotsky's observations about foreign language learning. After all, in the chapter in which these passages appear, Vygotsky was using the Tolstoy passages to begin to develop his case for a *dialectic* approach to concept development – a dialectic between affect and the inner workings of the mind on the one hand, and learning and instruction on the other. In it, he is working against Tolstoy's apparent determination (on account of his observations about attempting to teach his pupils literary language) to abandon direct teaching. 'What the child needs [wrote Tolstoy] ... is a chance to acquire new concepts and words from the general linguistic context' (Vygotsky 1962/1988:83).

In the 1988 edition of *Thought and Language* the Vygotskian text expands on this.

> It is true that concepts and word meanings evolve, and that this is a complex and delicate process. But Tolstoy is wrong when he suggests abandoning any attempt to direct the acquisition of concepts and calls for natural unhindered development. *Suggesting this, he divorces the process of development from that of learning and instruction.* (Vygotsky, 1962/1988:131, my italics)

Now we can see the apparent opposition of first and foreign languages which Vygotsky seems to establish. It is there in that revealing aside in the Tolstoy section and later in the description of the processes of foreign language learning as a school subject. But the opposition is not substantial. It is there by way of demonstrating the genuine need for teaching and learning to be treated as a unitary thing, to be seen as containing

131

developmental pathways that move both in an inward direction and outwards; complementary to each other – not in opposition and with development and instruction going hand in hand. 'All our evidence supports the hypothesis that analogous systems develop in reverse directions at the higher and the lower levels, *each system influencing the other and benefiting from the strong points of the other*' (Vygotsky, 1962/ 1988:110, my italics).

It is this dialectic that is the true legacy of Vygotsky's thinking, along with his methodological analysis and his reconstruction of the integrative relationship between development and instruction. That Vygotsky, in using schooled foreign language learning as an example of conscious learning, left the teaching methodology uninspected is not surprising given the history of pedagogy at that point. But this should not be our position. In multilingual classrooms where pupils are also learning English as an additional language, uninspected pedagogies are dangerous to learning – as are the uninspected pedagogies employed in foreign language classroom teaching. In both contexts, a generative interrelationship between need, experience and instruction needs to be established from the start. The additional language learning, foreign or otherwise, should not be being viewed primarily as based in conscious, academic learning which, when set alongside the so-called unconscious acquisition of first languages is, by inference, open to interpretation as being in opposition to it. Moreover, it is not the case that gaining skill in an additional language is absolutely dependent on prior skill in the first, that concept development is attainable virtually exclusively through one's first language.

We can speculate that had Vygotsky had the benefit of the hindsight granted us by virtue of our working with and building on his interactive, socially based theory of intellectual and skills development, and his illuminating concept of the zone of proximal development, he may well have made problematic, as we do, the disembedded teaching tactics which he seems to take for granted as necessary to higher concept development.

The fact is that the cognitive benefits Vygotsky so rightly claims for knowing more than one language are not lost when they are communicatively learned; learners remain conscious that they are learning to use a language and they are able to reflect upon that learning. The surface features of the target language (grammar, pronunciation, etc.) are still evident to learners. Communicative language development is not seen as excluding knowledge about language or grammar learning but rather as containing these strategies. Transfer of meaning from first language into second still obtains as a genuine strategy for learners, alongside other strategies. Crucially, the dialectic pathways of development are not lost in developmental pedagogy. Rather, they are enhanced.

Consequently, if multilingual classrooms are to fulfil their enriched potential for the learning of English as an additional language for bilingual pupils, it is essential that teaching practices are framed within Vygotsky's general theory of the social basis of learning, and not based upon extracted comments of his that seem to support disembedded, separate development – approaches long associated with classroom foreign language learning, and other unholistic approaches to education.

Note

The section in this chapter, 'Race and class prejudice and the educational offer in multilingual classrooms' is based on Levine (1990) 'Bilingual learners in English schools', in *Newsletter* No. 37, Autumn 1990, The British Association of Applied Linguistics.

References

Bourne, J (1989) *Moving into the Mainstream: LEA Provision for Bilingual Pupils*, NFER-Nelson

Chomsky, N (1965) *Aspects of the Theory of Syntax*, Cambridge, MA, Massachusets Institute of Technology.

Corder, S P (1967) 'The significance of learners' errors', *International Review of Applied Linguistics* 5(5)

Corder, S P (1971) 'Idiosyncratic dialects and error analysis', *International Review of Applied Linguistics* 9(2)

Department of Education and Science (1988) *Report of the Committee of Enquiry into the Teaching of the English Language* (the Kingman Report), HMSO

Department of Education and Science (1989) *National Curriculum Proposals for English for Ages 5 to 16* (the Cox Report, Part 2), HMSO.

Halliday, M A K (1969) 'Relevant models of language', *Educational Review* 22 (1), University of Birmingham

Halliday, M A K (1970) 'Language structure and language function', in J. Lyons (ed.) *New Horizons in Linguistics,* Penguin

Halliday, M A K (1971) 'Language in a social perspective', *Educational Review* 23(3), University of Birmingham

Hymes, D (1971) 'On communicative competence', in J B Pride and J Holmes (eds) *Sociolinguistics*, Penguin

Levine, J (1972) 'Creating environments for developing communicative competence: an approach to making foreign language-learning materials', unpublished dissertation for MA in Linguistics for English Language Teaching, University of Lancaster

Levine, J (ed.) (1990) *Bilingual Learners and the Mainstream Curriculum*, Falmer

London Association for the Teaching of English (1989) *Responses to English from Ages 11-16,* London Association for the Teaching of English

NCC (National Curriculum Council) (1991) *Circular Number 11: The Needs of Bilingual Pupils,* National Curriculum Council

Richards, J (ed.) (1974) *Error Analysis: Perspectives on Second Language Acquisition,* Longman

Selinker, L (1972) 'Interlanguage', *International Review of Applied Linguistics* 10(3)

Vygotsky, L S (1962/1988) *Thought and Language*, 2nd edn, Cambridge MA, Massachusetts Institute of Technology

Vygotsky, L S (1978) *Mind in Society*, Cambridge, MA, Harvard University Press

Postscript

We called it `Mainstreaming'

It has been instructive to watch the compilers of the Handbook of Inspection for Schools (1993, 1995) jettison the descriptive, and now pejorative and politically sensitive term 'mixed ability teaching', in favour of the more neutral and abstract 'differentiation'. The change *does* safeguard for wider use an essential dimension of good teaching, but it obscures the history of the past twenty to thirty years and the labours of the teachers who pioneered differentiated teaching strategies to make good the promise of a 'secondary education for all'. Despite all the criticisms levelled at them, the successes of teachers and of schools over the past twenty years or so should be measured by the increase in parental and public expectation of pupil achievement, and in particular by the fact that it is now possible to apply common criteria for 'quality' across the whole school system through school inspection

Josie Levine's contribution to this process is considerable, particularly in raising expectations of bilingual learners by teachers through insisting on their continued access to education (in 'mainstream') even while they were learning or extending a use of English. This work both relied upon and further developed the practice of differentiation, but it also insisted upon the practical value of cooperative learning – for students and teachers alike. Her thinking is clear, even simple. Taking beginners in English out of the context for which they need to learn to use the language to create simulations of these contexts is wasteful of teachers resources and loses pupils time in the strenuous and meaningful educational environments. Again her success can be measured in the *inclusion* of bilingual learners in the assessment procedures of the National Curriculum. Josie's counsel to teachers to apply 'educational rigour' to their work and to that of their pupils (rather than seeking the mirage of uniform 'standards' even for those new to English) predated the National Curriculum. Educational rigour is formalised and systematised in its criterion referenced assessment arrangements, and its descriptive use of age-links. Though the gains in fairness and in reliability of such systems of assessment are obvious within education, they have yet to gain complete acceptance beyond it.

Equally wasteful is depriving developing bilinguals of the opportunity to hear and later join in classroom conversations in cooperative learning situations, by removing them to environments in which only the teacher can act as a language model for them. The benefits of co-operative learning are two-way, with bilingual learners contributing to the global awareness and apprehension of linguistic diversity necessary in the modern world. Such gains are in direct proportion to the degree in which the classroom widens to accommodate all pupils' learning needs. Increased breadth and professionalism are the gains from co-operative teaching with specialist language teachers. In addition to their helping subject teachers focus and exploit the language-learning opportunities present in their classrooms, 'ESL teachers' can often give advice on the pacing, staging and analysis of learning tasks so as to remove obstacles to learning for the general benefit while, quite often, providing incidental impetus for the professional and curriculum development of the classroom teacher.

If spelling this out now seems redundant, it was not so when *Scope, Stage 2* was published in 1972. The world of English education was then a very different place. English teachers taught the mother tongue, usually 'through' literature. Applied linguists taught those who intended to teach English language abroad. 'ESL pupils' were largely taught by 'returnee'

EFL teachers who seldom had the experience or status to challenge the schools they worked in. It all seemed self-evidently right to many, and Josie's penetrating and clear sighted vision went largely disregarded.

Josie worked with teachers in classrooms, and with her higher degree professional students in the English Department of the University of London Institute of Education, to develop learning styles which emphasised communicating meaning as much as language form and structure; she took a cross-curricular view; she promoted active learning and problem solving approaches in the classroom, while also encouraging problem-solving approaches to their own language learning on the part of developing bilinguals, and helping teachers provide skilful and timely intervention and feedback to learners including, when it fitted their needs, access to learning language systems.

The intellectual sources of these approaches were multi-disciplinary: Josie brought linguistic interest in function (Halliday) and Communicative Competence (Hymes), and a passionate interest in Vygotsky's 'zone of proximal development' (before Vygotsky was classified as a 'constructivist') – as rationale for 'apprenticeship' models of learning for both pupil and teacher. Her teacher-collaborators brought powerful new tools to subject learning from their academic disciplines and took her insights into many curriculum areas. English teachers using structuralist and postmodern perspectives as means of helping pupils from a range of language backgrounds to explore text, was only one of these areas of development, though publication through the London English Centre helped to gain recognition and protection for their work. How to gain publication rights for their work was one of the things Josie tried to teach teachers (along with colleagues at the Instituteof Education). Her failure to protect her own rights in this way is one of the major reasons for the publication of this book. Incidentally, Josie's experience also offers implicit advice to innovatory teachers to use terms other than context-embedded 'working titles' to describe their work, if they are to stake their claims as educational pioneers.

A colleague at the Institute of Education once admitted that she read Josie's JLD car registration plate as 'Josie Levine, Deviant.' Visiting schools, Josie was *not* deviant. She had taught P.E., too and was calmly accepting of school routines and expectations. One could rely on her not to upset the management. Much of her success at innovating from within schools lay in her positioning of herself with teachers and schools. 'Making like a radiator' (ie disappearing into the wall) was how she expressed her skill at observing classroom interaction without affecting its quality – until she had won a mandate to join in from both pupils and teachers.

Her colleague was right, though. In terms of professional pigeon-holing, Josie was, and remains, deviant. As an English teacher, her background in ESL and in applied linguistics caused suspicion, even hostility. As a promising apprentice applied linguist she deserted ranks to join teachers at the unglamorous end of the educational enterprise – in classrooms – putting her knowledge and skills at the service of working-class girls and boys of black, white and Asian origin and demanding that they be treated as learners and language learners with the right to learn, and the ability to succeed. Instead of editing learned texts or journals, she edited (sympathetically and creatively) a series where new writers wrote 'good reads' for those numerous adolescents not enchanted by the classics – authentic texts, indeed.

She was, and remains, even after her 'retirement' from higher degree supervision, committed to helping teachers perceive when their insights approach new theory, and in helping them to articulate and publish it, rather than 'investigating' it on her own behalf. This route brought her to value teacher action research, as a description of in-depth understanding derived by teachers reflecting on their own practice – for their own development, and sometimes for wider information. She was as aware as anyone of the static, ungeneralised, directionless quality of much published action research. Careful, detailed editing and knowledgeable contextualisation of the case studies in her *Bilingual Learners and the*

Mainstream Classroom (1990) create a model for the resonance and authenticity possible for this kind of work. But it is not a highly valued academic mode.

Because so much of Josie's working life was spent with teachers improving teaching and learning in classrooms, we called on her often for validation. Much of Josie's writing, in consequence, was published in the broadsheets and conference proceedings of teachers' networks. This work has made a practical difference to education, for example, in the evidence given to the Swann Committee by the group of teachers she convened in the Schools Council *Language for Learning* project, that turned it from a report on *underachievement* into one on defining the conditions for success for bilingual learners in English schools. But such commitment delayed her academic progress. Worse still, it allowed for the colonisation of her ideas by the very applied linguists who had earlier scorned them, as 'Communicative Teaching' – marketed around the globe as strategies for English Second Language Teaching. The labelling of these strategies as pedagogies for a specific (less advanced) group of English users does violence to Josie's central concern: that the abilities of all pupils as *learners* potentially or even actually equivalent to their mother tongue peers, can be recognised and respected if teachers finally see past the permeable barrier of the language they currently use.

The charge here is not that the writers of these books do not acknowledge their sources in perfectly ethical academic terms. Nor is it that Josie's work alone is treated in cavalier fashion. Rather it is that by ignoring the context, history and intentions of the way ideas were developed and tried out in real situations, strategies are given a prescriptive force and presumption of universality that belies their origins, and does not automatically fit the many diverse language situations that may be described as second and additional language learning. The textbook style of these presentations may also make it harder for local teachers in ex-colonial situations to trust their own professionalism and creativity and their power to transform them in new situations. Here in the Eastern Province of South Africa, for example, these compilations bring into disrepute many of the changes necessary in English teaching, while possibly enshrining the notion of different learning strategies for teaching language to different groups – above all what a post-apartheid schooling system most needs to change.

It is to be hoped that this book will make it harder for Josie's essential role in the development of 'Communicative Teaching' to continue to be ignored and that it will foreground again the questions about the context and provenance of educational innovation Josie is most interested in.

Jean Bleach, Grahamstown. May 1996

References
Department of Education and Science (1985) *Education For All* (the Swann Report), HMSO

OFSTED (1993) *Handbook of Inspections for Schools*, OFSTED

Schools Council (1972) *Scope, Stage 2*, Longman